102 Tips to Communicate
More Effectively Using PowerPoint

Increase your impact with ideas on
Structure, Slide Design, Content, and Delivery

Dave Paradi

Published in Canada and the United States
by Communications Skills Press.

Library and Archives Canada Cataloguing in Publication

Paradi, Dave, 1966-
        102 tips to communicate more effectively using PowerPoint :
increase your impact with ideas on structure, slide design, content and
delivery / Dave Paradi.

Includes index.
ISBN 978-0-9698751-9-2

        1. Microsoft PowerPoint (Computer file). 2. Presentation graphics
software.
I. Title. II. Title: One hundred and two tips to communicate more
effectively using
PowerPoint.

T385.P36 2010   005.5'8   C2010-900466-3

Printed in Canada and the United States of America

www.102PPtTips.com

Cover artwork by Jordan Anastasi

PowerPoint® is a registered trademark of Microsoft Corporation.

Contents

Slide Design

Slide Content

102 Tips to Communicate
More Effectively Using PowerPoint

Increase your impact with ideas on
Structure, Slide Design, Content, and Delivery

Acknowledgements

In my last book, *The Visual Slide Revolution*, I thanked my audiences, colleagues in the speaking and presentation professions, and my family. And while some things change, some things remain the same.

I continue to be inspired and challenged by those I am fortunate to work with. The participants in my workshops who send me their current slides and ask for help with the slides that they are frustrated with. Newsletter subscribers who submit questions and slide makeover challenges. These people inspire me to deepen my expertise and thinking. And it benefits all future audiences and readers.

My colleagues continue to be shining examples of professionals who inspire me. The presentation professionals who make my jaw drop at their design and animation techniques that clarify complex ideas. The speakers who take communication and audience connection to new levels. I look forward to gathering with these colleagues every year at conferences and other occasions to share ideas and watch them demonstrate their craft elegantly.

And I continue to be blessed with a family that allows me to do what I do best. My wife Sheila provides valuable strategic insight and editing assistance in my work and also keeps our household running while I travel and speak. Our children, Andrew & Laura, understand the challenges of this work and are supportive even when my schedule gets crazy. Without my family, this book and my work would not be possible. They know how special they are and how thankful I am for their support.

Introduction

The term "Death by PowerPoint" is a common one in many organizations today. It refers to the use of the presentation software, PowerPoint, to communicate ideas in a boring or confusing manner. But PowerPoint presentations don't have to be that way. You can deliver PowerPoint presentations that communicate clearly.

I travel all over North America working with groups of presenters to help them become more effective when using PowerPoint. I have written over 200 newsletters sharing ideas to improve the presentations of thousands of people around the world. This is my passion and my audiences tell me that I have changed the way they use the tool forever.

While I was in New Orleans for a speaking engagement, I got the idea to collect the best ideas from my workshops and my writing, and format those ideas into tips that presenters can use to quickly improve the effectiveness of their communication. And that is how this book started.

The tips are organized by groups:

The first two tips: start here because these two are the most important tips

Structure & Sequence: the tips in this section help you plan your presentation for success

Slide Design: these tips help you create a design for your slides that is pleasant to look at and complements your content

Slide Content: from text to visuals to multimedia, these tips will increase the impact of your content

Delivery: tips to help you deliver your presentation in person, over the web, or by e-mail

Handouts: when you are using handouts, these tips will help you format and print them so that the audience keeps them and refers to them for years

The last tip: where to go for additional help on more technical questions about PowerPoint

You can read this book by diving in at any section you want to, but I recommend that you read the tips in order. I've sequenced the sections in the order that presenters should consider the topics, and I've sequenced the tips in each section to have a logical flow to them. Feel free to highlight certain tips or dog-ear the pages so you can find the ideas that appeal most to you.

While I do refer to PowerPoint in this book, the tips apply universally to almost every presentation software package or web-based presentation design and delivery tool. While newer versions of software sometimes alter implementation of techniques, I'm sure you'll find that the tips are applicable to any version of PowerPoint because they refer to the effective use of the tool instead of the "how-to" of the tool's features.

To help you apply the tips to your own presentations, I've created sample files in PowerPoint to demonstrate some of the tips. All of the sample files can be downloaded for free at Samples.102PPtTips.com. For each tip that has a sample file, you will see the following box:

> Sample file available at samples.102PPtTips.com

I have a number of how-to videos you can purchase at www.PPtHowToVideos.com that show you exactly how to use PowerPoint to accomplish a specific task. Where one of these videos applies to a tip, you will see the following box:

> Video available at www.PPtHowToVideos.com

The First Two Tips

Where do we start? With the two most important tips. I consider these to be the two most important tips because if you miss these, your communication is almost certain to be less effective. As you'll see in these tips, everything we do as a presenter should be about serving our audience.

Tip #1: Always ask yourself: How will this help the audience understand the message better?

This is the first tip because it is the one that should always be in your mind when considering any aspect of your presentation. Every element of your slides and everything you do in delivering the slides should be focused on helping the audience understand the key points you are trying to make. An effective presentation is one where the message is clearly understood and acted upon.

Whenever I am asked by a presenter whether adding a certain feature on their slide is a good idea or whether using a certain technique in their presentation is a good idea, I ask myself this question. It guides me in thinking about whether their idea will increase the effectiveness of their presentation. If more presenters used this approach, we would see less of the annoying aspects of presentations that lead to the conclusion that all PowerPoint presentations are poor presentations.

How can you use this approach? Any time you are tempted to add a photo, animation, funny video clip or any other element to your slide, stop for a moment and ask yourself if you are adding it because you think it is "cool", or are you adding it because it more fully explains your message and the audience will have an "Aha" moment because you added the element. As "cool" as some of these things may be, drop them unless they truly help the audience move towards the goal for your presentation.

Tip #2: Avoid annoying your audience

I truly don't believe that presenters deliberately set out to annoy their audiences. So why do so many presenters end up doing so? I think it is because they don't realize what annoys audiences. I've done a number of surveys of audience members and I ask them, "What annoys you about bad PowerPoint presentations?" I give them a list of twelve items to choose from and they pick their top three. Here's what they said in the latest survey.

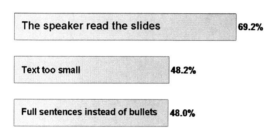

The speaker read the slides	69.2%
Text too small	48.2%
Full sentences instead of bullets	48.0%

548 respondents, October 2009

As you can see in the graph above, the single most annoying thing that a presenter can do is stand and simply read the slides word for word to the audience. It is even worse when they stand with their back to the audience and read the slides. This is simple to fix but so many presenters still fall into this trap because they do not allocate enough time to prepare their presentation and scramble at the last minute to throw everything they are thinking onto a set of slides. Since they don't have anything else to say, they simply read what is on the slides. You can fix this issue by planning in advance and giving yourself enough time to create persuasive visuals instead of a last-minute idea dump of text.

In the tips that follow, you will learn ideas on solving many of the other top annoyances. Keep in mind what your audience doesn't want you to do and you will steer away from the problems that plague too many presenters.

Structure & Sequence

I start every discussion about effective presentations with a focus on the structure and sequence of the information you want to present. Without a good structure and clarity of objectives, even the fanciest slides in the world won't save the presentation. These tips will help you structure your message, command the attention of the audience from the start, and end with strength.

Tip #3: Start with the goal of your presentation

Too many presentations end with the audience leaving the room wondering what the point was. They aren't sure why they just spent 30 or 60 minutes listening to a presenter who didn't seem to have any clear message. No action is taken, no change is implemented, no decisions are made, and it ends up as a waste of time for all involved.

The first step in making your presentation effective is to be clear on what you are trying to achieve with this presentation. What is your goal? We just need to look to nature to see examples of clear goals well executed. Take a shrub or tree. In the spring, its goal is to grow – spread its branches out, catch all the sun it can and be a strong, healthy tree. And it pursues this goal no matter what. It pushes through obstacles and shades out any ground plants that might want to steal its water or nutrients. You must be similarly clear about the need for a goal and its pursuit.

One way to get clear on your goal is to finish this sentence: "At the end of the presentation, the audience will _____." What will the audience know, understand, change, decide on, purchase, or take action on. This brings clarity to why you are doing the presentation and allows you to have a clear vision of the end state in the room after you are done the presentation. Without clarity of your goal, your presentation is likely to be less effective.

What if you struggle to finish the sentence above? What if you aren't really sure why you are doing this presentation? If this is the case, step back a moment. Consider who invited you to do the presentation. What problem, issue, challenge or topic did they want you to address? Why was it important for them to have you present? If you organized the presentation, think back to why you thought this was a good idea in the first place. What was motivating you at the time to want to share these ideas with this audience? It may be that circumstances have changed and a presentation is no longer the best vehicle for sharing the information with the audience. If so, it is perfectly OK to admit this and let everyone know that you'll be sharing the information in a different method that will be more effective for.

Tip #4: Every presentation is persuasive

If you think that your presentation is just an informative presentation that is not "selling" anything, I want to suggest that you still have an element of persuasion in your presentation. Sales presentations or those designed to convince the audience to make a certain decision are obviously persuasive presentations. But even presentations that inform or teach are persuasive because, as the presenter, you have to persuade your audience that the information you are sharing is valid and should be considered.

Most of us have been in a situation where a presenter delivers a "fact" and we immediately challenge it in our minds. We might think, "Where did they get that from?", or "I can't believe that is actually true!" Your audience may think those same thoughts unless you are able to persuade them that what you are saying is valid. You may need to cite the source, quote an expert, show an example, or share a story that proves your information is correct. When you do so, you are persuading the audience to believe your information.

Informative presentations also need to persuade the audience to consider and use the information being presented. What if the audience walks away from your presentation and never uses the information you presented – will your presentation be considered effective? Probably not. You need to persuade them to use the information, whether that is to apply the information in their own situation, consider the information when making a decision, or be aware of the information for possible future use. You may need to include examples of how the information can be used, what the next steps are, or when they should consider using the information you have presented.

Tip #5: Figure out where your audience is now

You should never give a "canned" presentation, one that is the same, no matter what audience you deliver it to. Why? Because each audience is different. As the presenter, you need to know where this audience is now if you are going to move them to the goal that you set for this presentation. In Tip #3, we talked about setting the destination for this presentation in terms of what you want the audience to do at the end of the presentation. As with any trip or journey, if you don't know where you are starting from, you won't know what route to take in order to reach your destination.

How can you determine where the audience is now? There are a number of dimensions to consider. First, find out who will be there. What is their position in the organization, what role do they play, what level of decision-making power do they have, and where geographically they come from. All of these factors can inform you as to whom you may need to pay more attention to in the room, since they are more critical to the success of your presentation.

Second, determine what their level of knowledge is on the topic. When thinking about knowledge level, consider both real knowledge and the level of knowledge they think they have – these two levels are frequently not the same. It is quite common that someone thinks they know more than they do. If you believe this to be true, don't embarrass them by pointing out the lack of knowledge. Incorporate phrases such as, "As you probably already know ..." to convey information without them losing face in front of their peers. If the audience on a whole has a lower level of knowledge than your usual audiences, this suggests that you may need to cover some of the "basics" at the start of the presentation so that everyone has the same knowledge before proceeding with more complex information.

Third, get a sense of their attitude towards your topic and your position on that topic. You may discover that some audience members do not like your topic area or are opposed to your viewpoint on the topic. Before a session in Jacksonville, I had a man approach me and say, "Just so you know, Dave, I hate PowerPoint!" I was clear on his attitude towards my topic! It allowed me to address some of the concerns that he and other audience members had at the start of the session, which diffused some of the tension, and allowed us to move on. You may need to do the same in your presentation.

Fourth, evaluate your level of credibility and trust with this group. If it is a group of colleagues you work with regularly, you may not need to address this issue at all because they know you. But if it is a group who has never heard of you or your organization, you will have to build credibility from the start. Build trust through your introduction and adding some information throughout proving that you are an expert in the field and worth listening to.

Finally, consider what style or format this group prefers for presentations. One of the industries I work with uses PowerPoint a lot but they never project their presentations. They only print the slides one per page and bind the pages along the long edge into a "flipbook." The presentations are done across a boardroom table with each person flipping through their copy of the book. It is important to present in the format or style that the audience is comfortable with to show that you are familiar with them and their issues.

Tip #6: Evaluate supporting information

When you find a fact, statistic, or example, especially if you find it on the Internet, how do you verify that it is true? Why should you even bother to verify it? Because if you don't, your presentation may not be successful. If you present a "fact" that the audience, based on their background or knowledge, knows is not true, they may doubt what you say and place little confidence in the rest of your presentation.

When evaluating data that you or others have calculated, always check the calculations. Perform spot checks of data that has been transcribed to make sure there are no errors. Check the formulas to make sure that the right components have been included and calculated properly. Do a reasonability test against other known data to see if these calculations fit a larger pattern. These checks and others that may be specific to your type of data are even more crucial when you are presenting something that is contrary to what has been accepted in the past.

When searching for information on the Internet, there are a few ways to assure yourself that what you are finding is actually true. First, look for the source of the data. If you read an article or fact that is not sourced, treat it with suspicion. A good author will always cite the source of the data so that it can be checked. When you see a source cited, see if you can go back to that source document to make sure that the author has used the data in the way that the researcher had intended and the data has not been taken out of context.

Second, when you find data or information online, make sure you evaluate the site it is coming from. I suggest you place higher value on sites that adhere to publishing standards. Sites such as those from educational institutions (.edu at the end of the

URL is one indicator of educational institution web sites), government sites, refereed academic journals and major newspaper or magazines all have standards that require articles to be independently verified before being published. While this is not an absolute guarantee of truthfulness, it at least assures you that some verification has been done and your risk of the information being fictitious is reduced.

Tip #7: Set out a map and follow it

The best way to make sure your presentation moves the audience from where they are now to where you want them to be at the end of your presentation, is to lay out a map of how you will make the journey. Share the map with the audience at the start of the presentation and follow the map throughout the presentation.

What should this map look like? It is quite simple and usually consists of the few major areas or points you will cover. The main points should be in a logical order so that the presentation flows smoothly from one point to the next without feeling like you are jumping around randomly. This map also keeps you on track and makes sure you are moving towards the intended destination.

I suggest sharing the map with your audience at the start of your presentation in the form of the agenda or list of key areas you will cover. This gives the audience an idea of how things will flow and they know what journey they are on. They can then consider each of the areas as a signpost along the route. Every time you move to the next area of your presentation, use a title slide to indicate that you are moving to the next topic. These title slides are the signposts the audience will be looking for and it guides them along the way.

During the planning stage of your presentation preparation, you should create a detailed map of your presentation. Start by deciding on the few key areas that you need to cover (these are the areas you will share with your audience). Then break down the key areas into the detailed points you will speak about using one of two effective methods: 1) use an outlining format in mind mapping software, or 2) use sticky notes or notecards to lay out the entire presentation under your main points. These breakdown methods give you a great visual way to see your entire presentation and make changes in sequence or add to areas that need more supporting information.

Now that you have a detailed plan of what you will present and the order you will present it in, you are ready to move on to consider how you will open the presentation, interact with the audience, and close the presentation.

Tip #8: Plan your opening

Experience tells us that if you do not grab your audience's attention in the first 60 seconds of your presentation, the chance of success drops dramatically. So how do you grab their attention? Not with a joke. Don't follow the outdated advice of starting your presentation with a joke. Unless you are a professional comedian who writes original material, you can be assured that someone has already heard the joke and it may not be very funny.

Instead, start with something unexpected that is related to the topic you are speaking about. Present a statistic that the audience is not familiar with that goes against conventional thinking. Now you have them curious about how this fact could be true when it doesn't fit with what they were expecting.

Another way to start is with a question that makes the audience think. Come up with a question that challenges their currently held beliefs or one that they can't easily answer. Then pause so they can reflect on their thoughts. Now you can start presenting your ideas and the audience will be engaged in what you have to say.

A third way is to start by telling a story that illustrates your theme or provides a real-world example of what you want to speak about. Stories are a good way to connect with your audience, and this starting story should be a strong one that gets people into the emotional mindset for what you have to say.

I start many presentations by presenting some original research or thoughts on my topic that are new to my audience. It immediately interests the audience because it is new information and gets us going into the topic right away.

There are many different ways to start your presentation, the above examples being just a few of the ways. The key is that effective presentations engage the audience intellectually and emotionally from the start. After you have their attention, then you can share the map of your presentation so they know where you are headed. By engaging the audience at the start of your presentation, the rest of the presentation flows easier because their interest in your message is already piqued.

Tip #9: Increase interaction with the audience

To engage audiences throughout your presentation, increase the interaction between you and the audience members. Most audience members don't want a one-way lecture style presentation, they want to play a role in the session.

One way to increase interaction is to get the audience's input on a topic where you capture their ideas in a document to be used or circulated later. Instead of using a traditional flipchart, hyperlink to a Word document in your presentation and capture the ideas so that everyone can see them and you have a document that is easy to e-mail or post after the presentation. This document could be action steps, items that need more research, challenges that need brainstorming to overcome, or any other list that will benefit the audience members.

If you are presenting calculated information, such as financial information where the inputs can change, show the changes by hyperlinking to a spreadsheet. Open a spreadsheet that has been set up with the inputs and calculations in advance. Ask the audience for input values and discuss how the conclusions change based on the different inputs. Show the effect of changing just one input and discuss how this might be accomplished. The spreadsheet moves the discussion from hypothetical to practical as the audience can see the impact immediately.

Instead of creating a presentation that runs from slide one to the end, create a non-linear presentation. After some introductory slides, give the audience a menu of topics you can discuss and ask them to tell you what topics they would like to hear about. Now you are truly making the presentation audience-focused because they are determining the content and sequence. This is easy to set up in PowerPoint and increases interaction because you ask the audience to vote on what topics are of greatest importance (if you have a large audience) or you simply ask a smaller group which direction they want you to go in.

Interaction during your presentation should not be accidental. It can be as simple as asking questions to start a discussion, or more advanced like the ideas in this tip. You should plan for it up front so that your audience gets the maximum benefit from the time they spend with you.

Tip #10: Write a description that encourages attendance

If no one attends your presentation, you don't have any chance of delivering an effective message. How do you get people to attend, whether it is a conference session, a community presentation, or a meeting at the office? I think that investing some time in writing an effective description of your presentation can result in a well attended session.

How do you write a description that convinces people to attend your presentation? Use the strategies that direct mail copywriters use. Presenters can learn from those who write the mail, brochures, or e-mails that sell products and services.

The first thing that copywriters would suggest presenters do is to get in to the mindset of someone who may attend your presentation. What topic or issue is of greatest importance to them right now? What pain are they looking to get a remedy for? What are they looking to learn that will help them in their job or situation? Note that this is different from the typical approach. Most presenters start from their own perspective and describe what they want to share.

Once copywriters know what the audience is looking for, they describe the session using language that clearly tells the potential attendee what they will get by attending. It can be one big promise or it can be a bullet point list that serves like a checklist for the potential attendee.

Notice how the focus is on the benefits for the attendee. As presenters, we need to have this audience focus in order to develop and deliver an effective description that encourages attendance and makes people look forward to your presentation.

Tip #11: Plan how you will follow up your presentation

Research published in the book *Brain Rules* by John Medina shows that people remember the information better if they are re-exposed to it after your presentation. This means that your presentation should consist of the time you have with the audience plus a planned follow-up to reinforce your message.

What does a planned follow-up look like? Here are a number of suggestions. You can plan to send one or more follow-up e-mails to the audience members to remind them of some of the key ideas, and direct them to more resources or implementation ideas. Write the e-mails in advance as you are developing your presentation. Double-check them after the presentation to make sure they are still valid based on the discussion in the presentation. A similar approach would be to prepare a special report extending the ideas and mail it to the audience members two weeks after the presentation.

If you want to take the next step, include multimedia in the follow-up. You can schedule a conference call or web meeting to answer any questions that have come up as the audience implements your ideas. Additionally, you can create a series of videos to reinforce your message or take the ideas deeper. These methods encourage the conversations from the presentation to continue and increase the probability that your ideas will be acted upon.

The follow-up for my presentations includes my newsletter which you can sign up for at **www.ThinkOutsideTheSlide.com** and my slide makeover video podcasts on my YouTube channel at **www.YouTube.com/ThinkOutsideTheSlide** (also available through iTunes).

Links available at samples.102PPtTips.com

Tip #12: Present your conclusion before your data

Research by Michael Posner, cited by John Medina in his book *Brain Rules*, says that our brains retain the overall meaning of an experience at the expense of remembering all the details. This means that the audience will remember the conclusion but not necessarily all the data that backs it up. That may be good for us as presenters because we want the audience to remember our key message.

The problem comes when that conclusion is buried deep in our presentation. Too often the typical sequence of a presentation is to present every supporting data point before we present the conclusion. By the time we get to the most important part, our audience is overwhelmed and may miss the conclusion or not recognize the significance of it.

I suggest that to improve the effectiveness of your presentations, start by stating the conclusion. Give the audience a clear idea of what the destination of this presentation is. Then you can support this conclusion with data presented in an order that logically supports the conclusion. Once they know where you are going, it is much easier for the audience to understand how the data you are presenting substantiates the conclusion you have already stated. And they remember that key message better because it was presented first and backed up second.

Tip #13: Consider the benefits of a non-linear presentation

I believe that the future of presenting is to create a non-linear presentation. In this type of presentation, you start with the overall conclusion, but then ask the audience what backup data or topics they would like to hear from a menu of choices you give them. The audience selects the topic that is most important to them at this time. When you have finished presenting that topic, you return to the menu of choices and allow the audience to select the next topic. The audience continues directing you until they are satisfied or have covered all of the choices on the menu.

This type of presentation totally engages the audience because they are in control of what is covered and the order. They may change their mind on what information they need to hear based on what you said in a previous section. They will end the presentation when they want to, satisfied that they have been given the information they need to act on your message. When the presentation ends may have nothing to do with how much time was allotted to the presentation at the start.

A non-linear presentation is built using the hyperlink feature of PowerPoint, which allows you to jump to any slide in the presentation. You design modules in the file and add hyperlinks that allow you to move between the menu and each module, then back to the menu. It does not require fancy programming, but it requires a little more planning.

Depending on the order that the audience chooses, you may need to recap some material at the start of each module. This helps the audience have the necessary background information for each module no matter what order the modules are presented in.

The first time you deliver a non-linear presentation, it can be a little scary. You are giving up control to the audience and have to be prepared to go wherever they want to go. But you will find that a non-linear presentation can be more effective because the audience is engaged and walks out knowing that they got what they came for.

Sample file available at samples.102PPtTips.com

Video available at www.PPtHowToVideos.com

Tip #14: Write your introduction with purpose

Far too often, the effectiveness of your presentation is undermined by a poor introduction. Why do poor introductions hurt your message? Because they take too long, they share information that is not important to the presentation and they have the wrong focus. I suggest that whenever you are being introduced before a presentation, that you write your own introduction and ask it to be read as written. Here's what I think should be in that introduction.

The first priority of your introduction is to share with the audience why they should listen to you. The introduction needs to overcome the skepticism they have as to why they should spend their valuable time listening to you. You need to build credibility in the introduction. Don't list every award or degree you have earned. The audience doesn't want your life history. They want to know what significant results you have produced, what degrees, designations or certificates you have that are relevant to the topic, and what similar work you have done in the past that shows familiarity with these issues.

Next, your introduction should set the stage for your presentation. Explain why your topic is important at this time and how your presentation will benefit the audience. This does not need to be more than one or two sentences.

Finally, the introduction should invite the speaker to start. The entire introduction should be sixty seconds or less. The audience wants to hear what you have to say, not listen to an introduction drone on and on. Remember that an effective introduction is not about you, it is about the benefits and value you will deliver to this audience.

Link available at samples.102PPtTips.com

Tip #15: Plan and practice
multi-presenter introductions

When you are presenting with others in a multi-presenter session, how do you hand the presentation off to the next presenter? Unfortunately, the most common introduction sounds something like, "Oh, this is your slide Leslie; I guess it's your turn now." Does that set up the next presenter for success? No. And it reduces the effectiveness of the overall presentation.

In a multi-presenter situation, the introductions need to be even briefer than a single presenter because it will otherwise interrupt the flow of the overall presentation. The aim should be for 15 to 30 seconds or less. Here is an example:

"As compelling as the operational advantages of this initiative are, we know that you are also concerned about the financial impact of the work. I'd like to ask Simran to come and talk about the financial analysis she has done that shows how this project is a high return initiative. Simran has an MBA and has provided solid analysis that we have based our own decisions on for two years. Simran, walk us through this next section please."

There are a number of things to notice in this example:

1. There is a tie to the previous section. To give the audience context for why the next presenter should be speaking, the previous presenter needs to set up why the next topic is relevant and important at this time in the presentation.

2. It positions why the audience should listen by previewing the key point that the next presenter will be speaking to. This gets the audience primed to listen to the support for the conclusion that they have been given.

3. It positions the next presenter as the expert in the topic by explaining that they are the ones who have done the analysis and their advice has been relied on in the past. It also gives any relevant education or external qualifications. If external qualifications are not available, reference internal ones.

4. It invites the next presenter to start right away with the topic at hand. The audience does not want to have breaks in the flow, so they want the presenter to get right to the points they are going to share.

These introductions should be practiced and rehearsed in advance. Don't think that you can just "wing it" on the day of the presentation. You will forget a part or forget to introduce the person at all. Also, don't just stumble through a printed introduction. If you need to read it because you won't be able to remember it, include it in your normal speaking notes and refer to it just like you would refer to your notes for any slide you are delivering. It should seem natural and flow like all the rest of your points. You are the one who will convince the audience that the next presenter is an expert.

A key component to making multi-presenter presentations effective is to develop and deliver the introductions so they create a smooth transition for the audience from section to section. Prepare for this part of your presentation just as you prepare for the content you will be delivering. It will make your presentation more effective and show how well your team works together.

Tip #16: Be purposeful about using black slides

One of the most effective things you can do in a PowerPoint presentation is to use a black slide. That's right, have nothing on the screen. How can that be effective? Because you have the total focus of the audience. There is nothing competing with you and you can have greater impact with your key point.

A black slide is not something you randomly use, but it should be planned. Think about a spot in your presentation when you will tell a key story or you want to emphasize an important message. Plan to use a black slide for greater emphasis at that point.

There are two ways to use black slides in your presentation. You can create a black slide by drawing a black rectangle over the entire slide. This is the technique you use when you plan the black slide in-between two other slides. You advance to the slide, step to the front of the platform and deliver your story or key message. When you are ready to continue, advance to the next slide.

The other way to use a black slide is during the delivery of a slide. At any time while you are delivering the slide, you can switch to a black slide by pressing the "B" key. If you want to tell a story or emphasize a point in the middle of a slide, use this technique to blank the screen. You can even use this technique when you decide to answer a question or go in a direction the audience wants to go in that is not what you have on the slide. It removes distractions and allows both you and the audience to be totally present in the moment.

As counter-intuitive as it seems, sometimes the most effective slide is no slide at all.

Sample file available at samples.102PPtTips.com

Tip #17: There is no correlation between the number of slides and the effectiveness of the presentation

A common question I get asked in my workshops is: "How many slides should I have for an x minute presentation?" In the past, people would suggest one slide every two minutes. So, for a 30 minute presentation, you would have 15 slides. I consider that rule to no longer be applicable because it is a rule that applies to text slides that are used as speaker notes.

With persuasive visuals, you may use a slide for a few seconds or a number of minutes, it depends on what the slide contains and how you are using it. As an example, I saw the video of a sales presentation that used 155 slides in 35 minutes and the presentation was masterful. The presenter is the top salesperson in the nation. He used the slides at times like a movie clip, once going through eight slides in three seconds as he showed how a particular feature was built into the product.

In my presentations, I usually average more than one slide per minute. When I ask the audience afterwards how many slides I used, the typical guess is about one-third of the actual number. They don't feel that I was cramming slides down their throats at all. The pace is comfortable because a persuasive visual only makes one key point and then it is natural to move on to the next point on the next slide.

The effectiveness of your presentation is not measured by how many slides you use. It is measured by whether your audience understands and acts on your message. Persuasive visuals are more effective than slides full of text, so the old rule on number of minutes per slide no longer applies.

Tip #18: Don't end your presentation with a slide that says Questions??? Or Thanks!!!

In my opinion, the worst way to end your presentation is with a slide that screams, "Questions???" or, "Thanks!!!" When you end with a slide that says "Questions???", it suggests to the audience that you know you weren't clear and you know they should have questions on what you presented. With the last slide saying "Thanks!!!", it says to the audience that you are thankful that the audience showed up and did not leave. With either of these endings, you leave the audience in a state of doubt that you have confidence in what you presented. When I share this perspective with people in my workshops, they nod in agreement and say it is one of the best takeaways from the day.

So what is a more effective way to end your presentation? End assuming that the audience understood what you said and be ready to discuss what comes next.

If you are doing a primarily informative presentation, you can end with a slide that recaps the key points and a discussion of how the audience will use the information you have presented. If you are doing a primarily persuasive presentation, you can end with a summary of what you see as the next steps and invite the audience to discuss these with you.

The way you end your presentation is critically important to how the audience perceives the entire presentation. Don't end with a weak closing that leaves the audience doubting what you said and unlikely to act on your message. End strongly with confidence in what you said and a desire to see the audience take action on your ideas.

Slide Design

Once your presentation has been well structured, the next area to consider is the overall design of your slides. These tips will help you select colors with purpose, select fonts that are easy to read, and set up a consistent look for each slide which will make your presentation flow well visually.

Tip #19: Don't use the templates or themes that come with PowerPoint

PowerPoint comes with a number of templates or themes that are pre-designed with backgrounds, graphics, colors, fonts, and sometimes even animation. I suggest you pass on these and create your own simple design instead. Why? I have found that these designs are distracting and hard to use. Here are some of my concerns with these designs:

- The colors that are used many times don't have enough contrast, making the slides difficult for your audience to see or read.

- The background graphics are distracting and cause the audience to focus on the background instead of your content.

- The fonts in many of the designs are serif fonts, which are harder to read when projected, again making it more difficult for your audience to read what is on the slide.

- The background designs many times don't leave enough space for your content, squeezing out the most important part of the slide, your visual.

So what should you do instead? Create your own simple design that is clean and easy for your audience to see. The rest of the tips in this section give you ideas on how to make your slide design effective.

Tip #20: Understand the emotions that different colors produce in your audience

Research shows that different colors evoke different emotions when viewed by most people. This is important when selecting a background color for your slides, as this is the color that will be showing the most in the majority of your slides. This table summarizes the key findings on the emotions that common colors evoke.

Color	General Feelings Evoked
Black	Heavy, mournful, highly technical, formal, death
Brown	Earth, simplicity, outdoors
Blue	Peace, tranquility, trust, confidence, security
Purple	Royalty, wisdom, spirituality, mystery
Green	Nature, environment, health, reptiles, insects
Gray	Conservative, practical, reliability, security, staid
Red	Passion, excitement, love, intensity, heat, aggression
Orange	Warmth, expansive, flamboyant
Yellow	Optimism, happiness, idealism, imagination
White	Purity, reverence, cleanliness, simplicity

When selecting a background color, consider which color would enhance the message you are delivering. Many presentations about the environment, for example, use greens and browns because those colors are consistent with the emotions that the presenter wants the audience to feel about that topic. The most common background color has been blue because of the positive emotions it evokes.

These emotional connections with colors can also be important when selecting text or shape colors. For example, red is a very strong emotional color and should be used with caution since it can evoke a strong emotional response in two opposite directions (love vs. anger).

Selecting a color for different parts of your slide can enhance the effectiveness if you understand the emotions associated with that choice.

Tip #21: Choose colors that have enough contrast

The most important aspect of choosing colors for your slides is to make sure that the colors have enough contrast. Contrast is a measure of how different two colors are, and it determines how easy it is to see one color when placed on top of the other color. If the text color does not have enough contrast with the background color, the audience won't be able to easily see the text and won't be able to read it. The same issue occurs when selecting colors for graph elements or shapes in a diagram.

How can you be certain that the colors you choose will have enough contrast? Most presenters, like myself, don't have a design background and can't just look at two colors and know if they have enough contrast. It isn't enough to look at the colors on your computer screen. Laptop and flat screen monitors are far brighter than projectors and give you a distorted perception of how much contrast two colors have. Instead, be sure by using the international standard tests for color contrast.

A number of years ago, the World Wide Web Consortium (W3C) created a standard that tests the contrast between two colors. They developed it to help web developers create easily readable web sites. We can use these two tests to make our slides readable. Both tests are calculations that use the Red, Green and Blue (RGB) attributes of the two colors to determine if there is enough difference between the two colors.

I've made this easy for presenters by creating an online Color Contrast Calculator that allows you to test the difference between two colors you are considering for your slides. Just go to **www.ColorContrastCalculator.com** to use this tool. The page also contains detailed instructions on how to find the RGB attributes of a color and some ideas on what you can do to improve the contrast of two colors if they don't pass the tests. You can also use this tool as an objective viewpoint when discussing color choice with colleagues.

Now you can make sure that when you are choosing colors for text, shapes, callouts, or graph elements, your audience will be able to see them easily.

The Color Contrast Calculator at
www.ColorContrastCalculator.com

Color Contrast Calculator
This calculator will determine whether two colors you are thinking of using on your slides have enough contrast to be seen clearly by the audience. The calculations are based on international standards developed by the World Wide Web Consortium (W3C). There are two tests, a color brightness test and a color difference test. Both tests should be passed in order to ensure that the colors you are using on your slides will be easily seen.

How To Use the Calculator
In the form below, enter the background color red, green and blue attributes and the text color red, green and blue attributes. The text color could also be a color you are considering for lines or shapes on the slide. You can find the red, green and blue attributes of a color by clicking on the Custom tab when you are picking colors (click here to view a PDF file with detailed instructions in a new browser window). As you change the attributes, you will see the sample automatically update. When you are done, click the Check Color Contrast button and you will see the results of the tests. The results give you a Pass or Fail rating as well as the value of that test so that you can compare it to the standard.

Enter Background Color Attributes:
Red: 1   Green: 0   Blue: 0

Enter Text Color Attributes:
Red: 0   Green: 0   Blue: 0

Check Color Contrast

Sample Text   Passed Brightness Test (>125)?   Test failed?
Passed Color Test (>500)?   Click here for suggestions.

Link available at samples.102PPtTips.com

Tip #22: Choose fonts that are big enough for the room and screen size

One of the questions that comes up often in my workshops is, "How big of a font should I use on my slides?" The only truly correct answer is ... "It depends."

I've heard a variety of answers to this question from different experts. Some quote a particular point size and some use ratios depending on certain parameters. I am sure you would agree that the text should be larger than the record for smallest font used on a slide that I have seen – Five point! I had to enlarge the slide just to see it was text instead of a thick line.

To properly answer the font size question, I did the research to come up with a way that I could determine an appropriate font size. I started by considering visual acuity. This is the term used for how well we see. It is what the optometrist measures using the eye chart that starts with the large "E" at the top and smaller lines below. They determine your visual acuity based on how tall a letter you can clearly see at what distance. It is important that we have the letters on our slides large enough so most people can see them.

The next challenge was to figure out what level of visual acuity I should assume for most audiences. To answer the average vision question I turned to the standard used for road signs in North America. There is a manual for designers of road signs that specifies how big the letters should be in order for the text to be read at a certain distance from the sign. So I used these standards and the visual acuity measurement standards to determine that road signs assume approximately 20/35 vision (20/20 is perfect vision). So, to be conservative, I assume 20/40 vision. It is one of the standard measurements and means that someone with 20/40 vision needs to stand 20 feet away from an object to see clearly what someone with perfect vision can see standing 40 feet away from the object.

I then used a projector to calculate the ratio of height of a standard Arial font to the width of the projected image. This allows me to know how tall a letter of a particular point size will be on a screen of a certain size.

Using the assumptions of 20/40 vision and that the image fills the screen, I could calculate the maximum distance that an audience member should be to comfortably read a font of a certain size. Now I can answer the font size question based on research, not on a feeling. There is no one single answer, it depends on screen size and the distance of the furthest person in the room.

What I have done is put all of this work into an easy to use table that is available for you to download for free from my web site. Go to **www.ThinkOutsideTheSlide.com/fontsize.htm** and you will see the link to download the table in Adobe PDF format. You are free to tell others about the link and encourage them to use it to make sure that their audiences will be able to read the text on their slides.

If you want a quick answer that will work most of the time, I suggest 36-44 point fonts for slide headlines (titles) and 24-32 point for main slide text. I'll sometimes use 18 or 20 point text for graph labels or callout text, but this is about the smallest text that works in most of the rooms I present in.

Link available at samples.102PPtTips.com

Tip #23: Choose a sans-serif font

Does the font face you choose matter? Absolutely. Research shows that when it comes to projected presentations, a sans-serif font is best.

Let's start by defining the two types of fonts that you would use. A serif font has little tails at the start and end of the letters, these tails are called serifs. They aid in reading because they help the eye to flow from one letter to the next. This text is in the most common serif font, Times Roman. This is the type of font that printed documents, like newspapers and books use. A sans-serif font does not have the serifs. The title of each tip is in the most common sans-serif font, which is Arial.

Designers who come from a print background will tell you that serif fonts are best because they are easier to read. While this is true for printed material, it is not true when it comes to projected presentations.

Research has shown that when projected, sans-serif fonts are easier to read than serif fonts for three reasons. All three are related to the fact that projected text is much lower resolution than printed text. The first reason is that the lower resolution makes the serifs jagged and they lose the advantage of smoothly flowing the eyes from one letter to the next. Second, the different stroke sizes that are used in serif fonts, especially the thin strokes such as the vertical strokes on a capital "N", are harder to see at a lower resolution. And finally, a sans-serif font is wider at the same point size than a serif font, making it easier to see at the lower projected resolution.

For these reasons, I suggest you choose a sans-serif font, such as Arial or Calibri for the text on your slides. Use a serif font only at larger point sizes and when you want the text to stand out, such as when quoting someone.

> Sample file available at samples.102PPtTips.com

Tip #24: Choose a filled bullet

When you are using bullet points on your slide, your choice of bullet character is important. I suggest you choose a filled bullet that is large enough to distinguish one point from the next. A filled bullet instead of a hollow bullet or hyphen gives the audience a better chance of seeing where each bullet point starts. A hyphen or a hollow bullet point character has a thin line that can sometimes get lost when projected. Without the bullet point to separate the points, the audience can think two points are actually one.

If you are thinking of using a graphic symbol or graphic image as a bullet point, consider if this is really such a good idea. I have seen presenters think they were being cute by using a logo or a symbol such as an airplane as a bullet point because they thought the audience would think it was really neat. Unfortunately, most of the time the audience can't figure out the graphic and they are distracted by the symbol, meaning they pay less attention to what is being said.

The best bullet point characters in my opinion are the filled circle and the filled square. They have enough presence to do what a bullet point is supposed to do for the audience. Make the size of the bullet character the same size as the text. This way, the bullet point is not too small that it disappears and it is not too large as to stand out and draw attention to itself.

Sample file available at samples.102PPtTips.com

Tip #25: Brand your slides

Branding is critical for communications. It helps the audience recognize who we are and who our organization is. Branding on our slides is achieved by placing our logo, web site or other branding on the background that is used for each slide.

Where should these elements go? My opinion is that they should go at the bottom of the slide. Why? It has to do with the way most screens and projectors are set up.

Too often, the image on the screen is quite low because the screen is mounted too low. This causes the people at the back of the room to not be able to see the bottom 10-15% of the screen due to the heads of the people in front of them. If you put your branding at the top of the slide, it pushes your content to the bottom of the slide, and into the region where some may not be able to see it. It suggests that the branding is more important than the content.

By placing the branding at the bottom of the slide, it is still there, but it is more subtle. It allows the most important part of your slide, your content, to be higher up and more easily seen by everyone in the room.

I don't suggest putting a watermarked logo behind the content as a way of branding. It distracts from the content on top of it and since it is washed out, the audience spends time trying to figure out what is behind the content instead of listening to you and your message.

With your logo or other graphics, use a file that has a transparent background. If you use a common JPG file, you will see a white box surrounding the graphic because a JPG file does not support transparency. Instead, use a PNG file that does support transparency and the graphic will look clean on the slide background. I would suggest that you have a maximum of three branding elements on your slides. The most common are your logo, tag line, and web site or toll-free number. By branding your slides this way, if a slide is printed out or passed on to others, the recipient will know who it came from and how to contact you.

Even if you are using a standard corporate template for an internal presentation, include your own personal branding such as your department name or division intranet address.

Branding is another element that adds to the effectiveness of your presentation.

Tip #26: Set up the Slide Master properly

The previous six tips have given you suggestions on the design of your slides. How do you make sure that each slide is consistent, so that the same colors, fonts and elements are on each slide in the same position? You set up the Slide Master. The Slide Master is where you define elements that will appear consistently on every slide.

I see many presentations where each color, font, and graphic has been added manually to each slide. Sometimes the colors are slightly different, the position or alignment of the title is different, or the logo seems to jump around from slide to slide. This is a classic sign that the Slide Master has not been set up properly. It also makes it very difficult to edit the slides or use the slides again in a new presentation.

After you decide on the content of your presentation, the first thing you should do in creating the design of your slides is open up the Slide Master and set the following elements:

- *Colors*: background color
- *Fonts*: font face, size, color, and alignment
- *Graphics*: lines, logos, and any other graphics that will be on each slide
- *Branding*: use text boxes to add tag lines, toll-free numbers, or web addresses
- *Menu hyperlinks*: for non-linear presentations, add a link on the Slide Master to be able to jump back to the menu from any slide

Don't get distracted by setting the "look" of the slide each time you create a new slide. Set up your Slide Master first, then focus on creating the content of each slide that makes your presentation effective.

Tip #27: Lay out your slide so it is familiar

If we want our audiences to understand and act on our message, we need to make our slides easy to interpret. One aspect of this is to lay out the information in a way so that the audience isn't searching for what they need to see.

The headline of your slide, many people refer to this as the title, should be at the top of your slide. If it is anywhere else, the audience will spend time finding it and not be paying attention to what you are saying. The title should be left-aligned or center-aligned, not right-aligned. Right-alignment is very difficult to read and causes the audience to do more work to interpret your slides.

The bottom of your slides is where the branding will go and other navigational information such as a tracker, which shows what section of the presentation you are currently in. This information should not go at the top, as that would give it too much prominence and take away from the more important headline and content of your slide.

The middle of the slide, the largest area, should be reserved for your content – graphs, diagrams, images, videos, or text. You want the audience to quickly focus on this as the key support for what you are saying. Don't distract the audience in this part of the slide with background images because it will reduce the time they spend understanding your content.

For pre-set positioning of elements on the slide, use the Slide Layouts that PowerPoint provides. When you add a new slide, it automatically asks you what layout you would like to use. Unfortunately, many presenters use whatever the default layout is and end up deleting the pre-set content areas if they don't need them. This causes many problems later on when applying a new

Slide Content

This section contains more tips than any other section because what you put on your slides is critically important to how effective your presentation will be. These tips range from text slides, to visuals, to specific techniques that will save you time, to animation, and to re-using slides from others in your presentation.

design or using the slide in another presentation. Instead, use the layouts as follows:

- *Title Slide* – use for signpost slides that indicate to the audience that you are moving to a new section in the presentation
- *Title only* – use for slides that have a headline and a visual such as a graph, diagram, image, or media clip
- *Title and text* (the default) – use only for bullet point slides; don't use this layout if you are going to delete the text placeholder, use another layout like Title only instead
- *Blank* – use for visuals that will cover the entire slide and don't need a headline

Sample slide design with branding at the bottom and areas for the headline and content:

Area for headline

Area for content

www.ThinkOutsideTheSlide.com

Tip #28: Use slide numbers only when necessary

Too often presenters put the automatic slide number in the lower right corner of the slide without thinking of whether it is necessary or not. I have found that most presentations don't benefit from the slide number. The slide number does not add to the audience experience of the presentation. There are a few uses for the slide number and you should consider whether you really need the slide number before adding it to your slides.

One of the uses for slide numbers is in presentations where you are not controlling what the audience sees. This can happen when you are doing a flipbook presentation (where the slides are only printed and bound in a flipbook, not projected), or when you are doing a remote presentation where the audience has a copy of the slides and is advancing them as you speak over a telephone connection. In these cases, slide numbers help the audience because you can quote the slide number to make sure that they are looking at the correct slide.

Another use for slide numbers is that they allow you to create a non-linear presentation. One of the ways to move through a non-linear presentation is to jump to the desired section by typing in the slide number of the first slide of that section and pressing the Enter key. By having the slide numbers on the slide, you will know what section you are in and when to go back to the menu or another section.

A third use for slide numbers is if you would like the audience to ask questions at the end and want them to be able to refer to a specific slide that they had a question on. The audience can jot down the slide number and their question so that at the end you can jump to that slide to answer the question.

If you are unsure of how much you may be your presentation, slide numbers may be helpful where you are during the presentation and h material you still have. If you have 40 slides half-way through your time you are only on sl decide to cut some information or speed up the pa ahead of schedule, you can introduce a discussio you don't finish too early. If you are using the slid this purpose, make the number a color that is audience to see so that the number is not promine only visible because you know where to look for it.

I am sure that there are other specific uses for s that you may encounter as a presenter. The impor that you think through why the slide number shot instead of just defaulting to always have it on the slid

Tip #29: Use testimonials to persuade

Professor Robert Cialdini documented the six principles of persuasion in his book *Influence*. The third principle is the Principle of Social Proof, which states that, "One means we use to determine what is correct is to find out what other people think is correct." We know this is true because we ask our friends or check online opinion sites when we want to find out about a new movie, a restaurant, or a vacation spot. We want to know what others, like ourselves think.

When you are looking to persuade your audience, using testimonials is one of the most effective approaches because it leverages this principle. What makes a testimonial effective in a presentation? Here are a few attributes.

First, it must come from someone similar to your audience. The audience places much more trust in someone that they feel is just like them instead of someone they can't relate to. Find someone who is in a similar role, a similar geographic region, in the same circumstance, or who had a similar objection to your proposed idea. When the audience says, "Hey, that person is just like me", you know you have the right person for a testimonial.

Second, make sure the testimonial is specific instead of generic. Your audience has heard so many "It was great" comments about every idea that they discount generic statements. What the audience needs to hear is that the person was in their shoes and here's how your idea specifically helped them achieve better results. The circumstance needs to be specific so that the audience recognizes the similarity with their own circumstance. The results must be specific so that the audience is convinced of the truth of the statement.

Next, keep the testimonial short. Aim for 60 seconds or less when spoken or one paragraph when written. Your audience will lose interest with a long-winded story.

Finally, when you use a testimonial, I suggest you have the following preference for formats. The best is to have a video testimonial because the audience can see the expression on the face and it is most believable. Next best is an audio testimonial played when a slide with a picture of the person is on the screen. Hearing emotion in the voice is powerful if a video clip is not possible. The final choice is a written testimonial. It is less effective when you have to read the words or let the audience read the quote on a slide, but it is still better than no testimonial at all. If possible, put a picture of the person on the slide with the quote.

Use the power of a testimonial to improve the effectiveness of your presentation.

Tip #30: Learn how to tell a story well

The one part of your presentation that the audience remembers more than any other part is the stories you tell to illustrate the points you are making. They can be personal stories, real-life examples, or even news stories. Years after a presentation, people will come up to you and recall a story you told even if they don't remember anything else you said. Because stories are so important, you should learn how to craft and tell a story well.

There are many books on storytelling and all of them present a structure for a story. Some are more complex than others, but all have most of the same basic components. I have enjoyed books by Doug Stevenson and I think his Story Theater Method™ is a good structure to follow. I suggest you read one or two books on telling great stories to see the way they suggest to structure and deliver a story.

Here are some tips I've picked up along the way. First, be clear on why you are telling this story. Spend some time thinking about the story you want to use and why you think it should be told. It must help move the audience along the path to the goal of your presentation. Don't tell a story just because you like it. If it doesn't have a salient point at that spot in the presentation, leave it out.

Second, plan how you will tell the story, don't wing it. Too often presenters try to wing it and it never works as well. There is a reason that there are so many books on storytelling – too many people don't do it well. Find a book that you like and follow the advice on planning the story. Rehearse telling the story and work on making it the best it can be.

Finally, if it isn't working, drop it. There are stories that I thought would be ideal, but the audience just did not respond well to it. So I dropped the story. Pay attention to the audience reaction when you tell the story and, if they are not responding, go back and work on the story. If it still doesn't grab the audience, let the story go. As presenters, we are a good judge of what the audience needs, but we are never perfect. Sometimes it just doesn't work and we need to recognize that fact and move on. Don't leave a story in your presentation hoping that more people will connect with it. Leaving in a poor story reduces the effectiveness of your presentation by confusing the audience or causing a low point in your presentation. Your presentation will be more effective when you use only those stories that connect well with the audience.

Tip #31: If you want the audience to remember what you say, figure out what it means to them

Research by Michael Posner concludes that people remember what they see and hear if they know why that information is important to them. Too often, presenters know why the information they are presenting is important, but they don't share that with the audience. They assume that the audience will know already or will easily figure out the importance. If the audience doesn't know or figure out the importance, the presentation isn't as effective.

As a presenter, it is your job to determine what your message means to your audience members. It is your responsibility to look at the information from their perspective, not yours. Then you will be able to communicate why the audience should listen and pay attention.

Each audience member reaches an "Aha" moment when they realize how the point you are making applies to them. It is at that moment that the audience member locks the information in their brain, and there is a much better chance at the information being recalled later and acted upon. This is important for both informative presentations, where you want new skills used later, and persuasive presentations, where you want key ideas used to make a decision.

By taking the audience's perspective, you will develop content that is more effective at communicating your message.

Tip #32: Use the Glance-Absorb-Return principle when thinking about bullet point slides

I don't think we need to eliminate bullet point text slides, but we need to make them more effective. When thinking about the text you will use on a bullet point slide, keep the Glance-Absorb-Return principle in mind. Let me explain what that is.

If you look at road signs, they are always easy to see and understand quickly. They need to be so that drivers keep their focus on the road and the surrounding vehicles to avoid accidents. If you had to read a paragraph of text on a road sign while driving, you'd lose the focus on the road and end up crashing into the vehicle in front of you or running off the road.

They design road signs so that you can Glance at them, Absorb the information in about a second to a second and a half, and Return your focus to the road. Hence my Glance-Absorb-Return principle. It applies to text slides as well. The audience should be able to Glance at the text you have put up, Absorb the key point in under two seconds, and Return their focus to hear you expand on what the bullet point said. Here are some ways you can apply this principle on your text slides.

First, always use bullet points instead of full sentences. A bullet point shares just the key idea or concept and is not everything you are going to say on the point. Second, use the six by six guideline when creating bullet point slides. This guideline suggests no more than six words in a bullet point and no more than six bullet points on the slide. It helps focus the text you use. Finally, use animation to build each bullet point on the slide so that the audience can glance at the new line you have just put on the slide and then return their focus to hear more.

Tip #33: Six ways to emphasize text

When you want to emphasize certain text in a quotation or bullet point, here are six ways to make those words stand out (and some caveats about using them).

1. Use Bold or Italic font – This method is easy to do because you just highlight the text, and apply the bold or italic font format. While it is easy, I have found that simply applying one of these effects does not always make the emphasized text stand out well from the normal text. Unfortunately, like many of the methods that involve formatting the text of the passage, it is not possible for you to build this effect through animation, so your audience may first focus on the emphasized text instead of the context.

2. Use Bold and Italic together – By combining both bold and italic together, the emphasized text does stand out better from the regular text. But it still can not be built through animation.

3. Use an Underline – Underlining is slightly better than the previous methods because it adds something outside the characters that pulls the eyes towards certain text. There are two ways to underline text. First is to use the underline font format, which will work, but cannot be built as you are speaking. The other way to underline is to draw a line object under the text you want to emphasize. Because this is a separate slide element, it can be built through animation. But the thin lines that are used are sometimes hard for people to see.

4. Color the text – By changing the color of the emphasized words, you make them stand out better than any of the previous methods. Remember to pick an emphasis color that has good contrast with your slide background so the emphasized text can be seen easily. But like most of the previous methods, this effect can not be built through animation unless you have a separate text box with the exact same text that appears over the passage. This is tricky to get perfectly lined up.

5. Use a semi-transparent box – This method works well whether the text passage is a text box, or an image of text on a page, such as captured from a PDF document. In this method, a rectangle is drawn over the text that you want to emphasize. Then you make the fill color semi-transparent, allowing the text underneath to show through. You will usually also have a line around the emphasis box for extra clarity. This separate element can be built using animation, so it has that advantage over most of the previous methods. The only downside is that sometimes the text underneath is hard to read unless you make the transparency fairly high. If you have a text passage that is an image, this is the best method.

6. Highlight the Text – Unlike Word, PowerPoint has no text highlight feature. In Word, you can simply select some text and use the highlight tool to see a yellow (or other color) background for just that text, similar to using a highlighter on a printed page. This feature does not exist in PowerPoint. But we can simulate it by placing a colored rectangle behind the text. You will now see the text emphasized with a different background color. You can animate this rectangle so that you can have the emphasis appear when you want it to.

I have used almost all of these techniques to emphasize text at one point or another in my presentations. Select the one that will work best for each situation to communicate your point most effectively.

Sample file available at samples.102PPtTips.com

Video available at www.PPtHowToVideos.com

Tip #34: Remember what has worked for 5,000 years

It helps to look at how we have effectively communicated in the past. Thousands of years ago, we drew on a cave wall and we used that drawing to communicate important lessons. The crude drawings told a story to all observers. Formal language was not yet in use, but traditions, history, and important lessons were still effectively passed on. Each of us can also remember how important stories and traditions are passed on in our own families. Many of us can recall sitting with a grandparent, uncle, or aunt and having them show us an old photo or yellowed newspaper clipping, telling us the tale of that day or event. So we know about visuals on a personal level and how visuals have been a powerful means of storytelling and communicating ideas for thousands of years.

So why is it that when PowerPoint was introduced, we forgot what has worked for 5,000 years and started putting paragraphs of text on slides and reading them to our audience? I can't figure that one out. PowerPoint is just a new tool to use when communicating, no different than paper was a new tool in its time. The same principles still apply today. To effectively communicate, craft a story that your listeners will be interested in and use visuals to help illustrate the story for them.

It is quite simple, and as presenters we need to be reminded that the principle that worked 5,000 years ago still works. It's not the tool you choose, it's how you choose to use the tool that makes the difference.

Tip #35: Use visuals instead of text whenever possible

Is it just me who suggests that visuals are more effective than text slides? No, research confirms these ideas. The first piece of research derives from Professor Richard E. Mayer's book, *Multimedia Learning*. Dr. Mayer is one of the most published and respected academics on the most effective use of media when presenting ideas. His principles of media design can be applied to the creation of persuasive visuals. The most important of these conclude that audience members understand better when we speak about a visual instead of simply displaying text that we (and the audience) reads.

The second research comes from Professor Allan Paivio. His Dual-Coding Theory of Cognition states that information is processed in two distinct channels in the human brain: one deals with visual information and one handles verbal information. The brain codes each type of information differently and we comprehend best when the visual and verbal information is consistent with each other. If there are multiple or conflicting inputs in a single channel, it leads to difficulty in interpreting the different inputs, since they compete with each other.

When we apply Professor Paivio's theory to business presentations, we recognize that a well-designed, clear visual that is explained verbally will result in the best understanding by the audience. Confusing visuals or reading text that is displayed will cause overload in one of the channels and leads to poorer results for our presentation.

The case for using visuals is irrefutable. It is based on research that has been consistently proven in academic circles.

Tip #36: Cut graphics costs

If you have graphics designed by a design firm, you may have run into the situation where the design firm charges a fee every time a minor change is made. Since most times the graphic is a single image, any minor change needs to go through the design firm, costing a significant fee, no matter how small the change. Here are some ways to better control these costs.

When you are contracting for some graphics to be designed for your slides, make sure you select a design or graphics firm who is willing to design the graphics in a way that you can make minor changes yourself or re-use parts on other slides. Ask them to provide the finished graphics as individual images grouped into the completed graphic. That way, if you need to make a minor change, you can ungroup the individual elements, make the change, and re-group them.

Another way to create professional graphics is to do them yourself using high-quality vector images. Combine individual elements and you can create the exact graphic you need. For example, you can combine a truck graphic and a factory graphic with one of a retail store to show the movement of goods through the process in your firm. Where do you get these vector images? I'd start with **istockphoto.com** and search for your keywords while specifying that the results should be vector images. I use some vector images from istockphoto in my own presentations.

Can you use professional graphics and not break the bank? Yes you can, by creating them yourself or leveraging the graphics created for you by a design firm.

Link available at samples.102PPtTips.com

Tip #37: Where to get ideas for visuals

Do you need graphics or design training to be able to come up with the visuals that work for the points you are making? No. I have no graphics or design background, so if I can do it, you can too. But sometimes we need a little inspiration by seeing what visuals others have created that stimulate our own thinking of how our information can be presented. Here are some places I go to get ideas for visuals.

www.visual-literacy.org/periodic table/periodic_table.html – The web site is a project from a group of academics who are studying ways to represent concepts visually. This page contains a large number of potential visual ideas organized into categories based on the periodic table of elements (there's the academic influence showing through). Notice that they have organized the visual methods (as they term them) by color to represent what you are trying to visualize (data, concept, strategy, etc.). They have added text colors and symbols to further categorize the methods on the basis of process vs. structure, detail vs. overview, and divergent vs. convergent thinking. It may seem a little too academic, but roll your mouse over any of the boxes in the table, and you will see a popup example of the visual relating to that method. It is interesting to see some of the examples and it will give you ideas for your own visuals.

www.powerframeworks.com – A subscription site that has a large library of already created slides using visuals to represent concepts. You subscribe to the site and can then download any of the ready to use frameworks as they call them. A good site for ideas and ready made graphics for your presentations.

www.billiondollargraphics.com – This site, by artist Michael Parkinson, contains ideas and products that help you design graphics. It is aimed at those who want to design more complex or higher end graphic images. See *www.billiondollargraphics.com/businessgraphiclibrary.html* for some sample ideas.

www.plays2run.com – An innovative site that discusses ways to influence others based on real world research. As you explore each of the play types, pay attention to the ideas given and consider how you may create graphics that illustrate the point you are making. Use this as a site to stir your creativity.

And, of course, for additional inspiration you can always use the more than 25 sample visuals in my book *The Visual Slide Revolution* (available at **www.VisualSlideRevolution.com**).

> Links available at samples.102PPtTips.com

Tip #38: Create persuasive visuals using the KWICK method

In my book *The Visual Slide Revolution*, I share my five-step method for creating persuasive visuals, what I call the KWICK method, since KWICK is an acronym to help remember the steps. Here is a short summary of the steps you can use to create and deliver persuasive visuals.

Key Point – Write a headline for each slide that summarizes the message you want audiences to remember

Words That Suggest a Visual – Use the clues in your slide headline, the words on your slide, and the words you say to determine which visual is the best for this point.

In Context – Create the visual so it is easy to understand and has context for the audience. Explain visuals such as graphs, diagrams, timelines, videos, and maps to "show and tell" instead of just "tell".

Crystal Clear – Use a callout instead of a laser pointer to make the point of the visual clear to the audience in the room, across the world via web presentations, and to those who will receive the presentation by e-mail later.

Keep Focus – Build each element on the slide so that you discuss one topic at a time.

Link available at samples.102PPtTips.com

Tip #39: Single numbers need to have context to give them meaning

If you are presenting a single number as the result of a measurement (such as a financial result or result of a specific test), don't just present the number. Why? Because if all you do is present the number, you assume that the audience knows how to put that number in context, which is not a good assumption to make. You need to give the number context in one of three ways so that the audience knows whether this number is a good, neutral, or bad news story.

The first way you can give the number context is by comparing it to the expected value for the measurement. The audience can compare the measured result to what was expected in order to determine the message.

The second way to give context is to compare the result to previous values of the same measurement, whether it is previous tests or previous timeframes in financial results. By seeing what the measurement was previously, the audience can see the change between the previous and current results and determine what the change means to them.

The third way to give the audience context is to compare the measured result to a standard value. If a standard exists based on regulation or industry expertise, the audience can derive meaning from seeing how the current result stacks up against the standard.

Presenting numeric results effectively requires a presenter to place the result in context so that the audience understands the message clearly.

Sample file available at samples.102PPtTips.com

Tip #40: Use copy and cropping to build a single graphic piece by piece

When you use a graphic that illustrates your point, it is most effective when you build it piece by piece so that you can provide an explanation along the way to the audience. But if the graphic has been supplied to you as a single image, how can you build it one by one? By using the copying and cropping technique.

Start by determining which pieces you need to create out of the whole image in order to build it piece by piece. For each piece, copy the entire image and use the cropping tool in PowerPoint to crop until only the piece you need is showing. Since the cropping tool in PowerPoint only crops in a rectangular shape, you may not be able to achieve a perfect result, but it is better than the confusion of showing the entire image and trying to use your finger or a laser pointer to explain the pieces.

Once you have the separate pieces, position them on the slide side-by-side so that they look like the original image. To do fine positioning, hold the Ctrl key and use the arrow keys to move the piece one pixel at a time. You may also need to move certain pieces backwards or forwards in the layers so that the image looks like you want it to (see Tip #55 for more on layers).

The final step is to build each piece using the animation feature. It usually works best to use a simple effect such as the Appear effect for building the pieces of a graphic. Now you will be able to explain each piece to your audience and your message will be more effective.

Video available at www.PPtHowToVideos.com

Tip #41: Align & distribute to make elements look ordered

When you have multiple photos, shapes, or text boxes on a slide, you may struggle as I do in lining them up perfectly in a row or column by hand. Isn't it OK if they are "close enough"? Unfortunately, no. People infer importance by position. What may be a small difference on your screen becomes a large difference when projected. The audience may interpret someone as the head of the team if their picture is slightly higher in a row than the other team members.

When positioning objects on a slide, people interpret objects that are closer together to be somehow related. So if you don't want to suggest a relationship that is not correct, you need to evenly position the objects across the slide vertically or horizontally. Doing this by hand is very difficult and too often does not work out the way you planned.

Fortunately for all of us, PowerPoint has two features, the align and distribute features, that automatically do this for us. I often use them to make creating slides simpler. When using these features, here's a trick I have learned. If I want a group of objects to be aligned with their right edges in the same spot, I will position one object exactly where I want the right edges to be. Then I position the other objects to the left of that one. When I use the right align feature, it lines up the right edges according to the object that is positioned farthest to the right, so I get everything lined up with the first object I placed in position.

When distributing objects, pay attention to whether you are distributing them within the space they already occupy (as you would for a timeline) or whether you want to distribute them across the entire slide (as you would for a group of pictures of team members possibly).

Here is an example of how I would use these techniques to create a Gantt chart timeline. First, I add text boxes with each of the time points, for example 0, 2, 4, 6, etc. weeks up to 18 weeks. I place the 0 and the 18 week text boxes at each end of the timeline. I use the align feature to first align all the text boxes so their tops line up. Then I use the distribute feature to evenly distribute them along the timeline.

By using these two features, you can save yourself a lot of time.

Sample file available at samples.102PPtTips.com

Video available at www.PPtHowToVideos.com

Tip #42: Use graphics software to resample photos before you insert them on your slide

When you add digital photos to your presentation, they can make the file size grow quickly and the presentation soon becomes too large to e-mail. The solution is to resample the photos so that they take up less space and still look good. There are two techniques to know about. This tip deals with resampling before you insert the photos on your slides and the next tip deals with resampling if the photos are already on your slides.

Resampling is just a technical term that refers to a mathematical technique for removing the pixels (or dots) from the photo that you won't be using anyways. Don't worry that it will reduce the quality of the image on the slide – it won't. Most digital photos have far more pixels than could ever be used by a projector or computer screen, and all we are doing is removing the pixels that won't be shown.

Before you insert the photo on your slide, you can resample the photo using graphics software such as Adobe's Photoshop or IrfanView. IrfanView is available at **www.irfanview.com** and is a simple alternative to a complex graphics program. It works extremely well for this purpose and costs much less than Photoshop does. It is the program I use all the time.

In the graphics program, you set the new resolution for the photo. First, make sure that the aspect ratio, the ratio of width to height, will be maintained so that the photo doesn't get distorted. In most cases, the maximum size of a photo for use in PowerPoint is 1024 x 768, which is the maximum resolution of many projectors. This selection will keep your image crisp and clear and your file size under control.

After resampling, always save the resampled picture to a new name so you don't overwrite the original photo that may be used in other purposes that require the higher resolution. I usually append something like 1024 to the end of the photo name so that it still sorts in the same order when I am looking at the list of files. In this way, I know the resolution of the file is 1024 x 768, and it is the one to select when inserting on my slide.

Link available at samples.102PPtTips.com

Tip #43: Reduce the size of your file by resampling photos in PowerPoint

If you have high resolution photos in your presentation that are making the file size too large to work with, PowerPoint does have a feature that will resample the photos from within PowerPoint. Why wouldn't I suggest only using this technique instead of the previous tip? Because I prefer the resampling to be done before I insert the photo on the slide – it seems to give better results for me. This tip is for those situations where the presentation is already done and you don't want to have to recreate it with resampled photos.

On any photo in your presentation, find the formatting option that allows you to Compress the picture. It will give you some options. You want to select the option to compress to Web/Screen resolution (don't worry about the dpi setting it shows, it doesn't mean anything for projected presentations). And select to do the compression for all pictures in the document so that you don't have to do this individually for each picture.

Once the pictures are compressed, you will see a difference in file size when you save the file. I have seen this technique compress a file up to 96%! Now the presentation file will be much easier to e-mail and will run faster.

Video available at www.PPtHowToVideos.com

Tip #44: Differences in using photos from the PowerPoint library and stock photography sites

When you use photos from the library that comes with PowerPoint or from a stock photography web site like **istockphoto.com**, there are a few key differences to keep in mind.

The PowerPoint photo library is accessed from within PowerPoint by searching for Clip Art. Even though there are not many photos loaded on your computer when you install PowerPoint, it can access the online library that Microsoft maintains. By selecting to search web locations as well as local photos, the PowerPoint search will locate photos in the over 150,000 item library on the Microsoft web site that is free for you to use. When you are searching this library, use only one word as your search term. This search seems to not find many, if any, items when you use more than one word as a search term. You can then directly insert the selected photo on your slide without needing to download and save it first, which saves time.

With commercial stock photography sites, you first have to go to their site in a browser. Their search engines work more like web search sites such as Google. The more words in the search term, the more likely you are to find exactly the picture you are looking for. When you have found the right photo, you need to purchase it and download it to your computer. You may have a choice of what resolution to buy. My suggestion is to purchase the photo in a resolution at least 1024 x 768 so that you can use it full-screen if you want to. After you have the picture file on your computer, you insert it in on your slide in PowerPoint by using the feature to insert a picture from a file.

I will usually search the PowerPoint library first before using a commercial stock photography site because it is less expensive, but I have used both in presentations many times.

Video available at www.PPtHowToVideos.com

Tip #45: Remove the background of an image to make it blend in with your slide

Photos or images that are saved as JPG files (the most common format), will sometimes have a white background because the file format does not support transparency. If your slide background is white, this usually is not a problem, but if the background is not white, you end up with what looks like a white box around your image. Most times the image will look better on your slide if it has no background since it will blend nicely and the white won't attract attention away from the image.

PowerPoint has a feature that may allow you to drop out the background from an image. When you select the image, there is an option to Set Transparent Color. This option gives you an eyedropper cursor. Move the cursor to the color you want to remove from the image and click. PowerPoint removes that color from the image.

Many times this will work, but there are cases where it won't work. If the background color is also part of the image, part of the image disappears as well. If the background is not one color, only some of the background will be taken away but some will still remain. In these cases, this technique will not work. You can use a graphics package such as Adobe's Photoshop to remove the background, but that requires additional software and the knowledge of how to use the package. There is another approach in PowerPoint you may want to consider.

Using the freehand drawing tool, draw a shape close to the edge of the image so that your shape covers the background only. This may require more than one shape and works best if you zoom in so you can draw the shape as close as possible to the part of the image you want to keep. Then, set the fill color of the shape to the Background option. This acts as if the shape and everything underneath it is transparent. The result is that the background of the image (or at least most of it) is taken away. If you are animating the image after using this technique, you may need to also animate the shape(s) covering up the background. You will likely need to experiment a little to see what it looks like. While this is a more involved process, it yields better results when the Set Transparent Color technique does not work. It is also easier than having to use a graphics package to remove the background.

Video available at www.PPtHowToVideos.com

Tip #46: A quick way to create a presentation of photos

If you are creating a presentation where most or all of the slides will be slides of photos, PowerPoint has a feature that can help automate the creation of the slides. To ease selecting the photos, put all of the photos in one folder on your computer. It is also best if you resample them before you start (see Tip #43 on resampling) so the resulting file won't be too large.

In PowerPoint, select the feature to insert a Photo Album. This gives you options to select which photos to create as slides. It also gives you options to set the layout for each slide so you can select which slides are full-screen photos and which have titles or even multiple photos per slide. You can adjust the parameters of the photo so it looks best. You can move photos up and down in the list so you can order them properly. You can even insert a slide that has a text box on it so that you can add section header slides to break up the presentation. After you have set the options for each slide, click the Create button to create the slide show.

Once the slides are created, you can edit them just like any other slide show. Add animations, edit the title or other text, add callouts, or insert other slides as needed. This method allows you to quickly create your presentation if it consists mostly of photos. Now you can better use the time you saved for practicing your presentation so it is as effective as it can be.

Video available at www.PPtHowToVideos.com

Tip #47: Explain how to interpret unfamiliar graphs before you show them

There are times when you will have to present graphs that are not simple, everyday graphs. It may be that you are showing some statistics that require error bars in addition to the data point. Or it may be that the graph requires a logarithmic vertical axis. In these cases, your point will not be effective unless your audience understands the graph.

If you are presenting to an audience of technical experts that deal with these types of graphs all the time, it won't be a problem. But what if your audience is made up of people who are not experts in the field or are media that will report on this information to the public? They will be confused by the graph because they don't recognize it. That confusion will lead to your message not being very effective or, even worse, they may misinterpret your message and come to the wrong conclusion.

In these situations, I suggest you start that section of the presentation by explaining to the audience how to interpret what they are about to see on the graph. If the data point will look different, it may help to enlarge one of the data values and explain what the data point represents and why the additional information is there. If the scale is the unusual aspect, come up with an analogy that the audience can relate to so they can place the scale in context. Armed with information on how to interpret the graphs, the audience will be more likely to read the graphs correctly.

Remember that it may be familiar to you, but those without your background will not understand what you are showing unless you first teach them how to read the graph.

Tip #48: Four ways to capture a screen

When you want to demonstrate a web site, show how to complete a form in Word, or use an example from any application, using a screen capture visual is the best way to show it to your audience. In many cases a screen capture is more effective than showing the web site or application live because there are many technical problems that can cause your demonstration to go awry. Also, there are too many other distractions in live demonstrations that take away from the key point you are trying to make.

There are at least four ways to actually capture the screen, depending on what software you have. The first two methods work in any version of Windows. By pressing the PrintScreen key (sometimes abbreviated to PrtScrn or something similar), Windows captures the entire screen and copies the image to the Windows clipboard, allowing you to paste it on your slide. If you want to capture only the current application, for example your browser without seeing other applications or the taskbar at the bottom of the screen, hold down the Alt key and press the PrintScreen key.

If you are using Windows Vista or Windows 7, it includes a Snipping Tool application under the Accessories list that allows you to draw a rectangle around the information you want to capture on your screen.

The gold standard, in my opinion, which gives you endless options, is a commercial program called SnagIt from TechSmith. It gives you a host of options on capturing your screen and editing it before placing it on the clipboard. TechSmith also makes a product called Jing that allows screen captures with less features, but it is free at **www.jingproject.com** (and it has a Mac version as well). So if the first three methods won't do exactly what you need, I suggest you try Jing or invest in the SnagIt software at **www.SnagIt.com**.

Once you have the screen capture on the clipboard, switch back to your PowerPoint slide and paste the image on the slide. It appears like any other image and allows you to apply the same editing as a picture would. I suggest you first crop the image so that only the important parts are showing. Don't distract the audience with parts of the screen capture that are not critical to your point, like scroll bars or extra toolbars. Then, size the resulting image to fill the available slide area as much as possible. This makes it easier to see for the audience.

After the image is on the slide and looking good, there's one more step. You need to make sure that the audience knows what area of the screen shot you want them to focus on. Add a callout that consists of a graphic highlight, such as an arrow or rectangle to show the audience where you want them to focus. Add callout text that explains why this one spot is important (see Tip #56 for more on callouts). Now you have a screen shot that is effective in showing your point to the audience.

Video available at www.PPtHowToVideos.com

Tip #49: Use the zoom-in technique to make screen captures easier to understand

The unfortunate thing about using screen captures is that too often the information we want the audience to see ends up being too small when looking at the entire screen capture. A good technique for making the information bigger while keeping it in context is to use the zoom-in technique. Here's how it works.

First, place the screen capture on your slide as you normally would, then crop and size it to fill as much of the slide as possible. Draw a rectangle around the key area on the screen capture that you will focus on. Copy the screen capture and crop it so that just that key area is shown in a new image. Size the new image to be large enough so that the audience can clearly see it. Place the callouts on this zoomed-in image of the key area.

Set the animation as follows. Show the entire screen capture first so that the audience has context of what you are discussing. Then, make the rectangle appear so that they know what portion of the screen capture you will be focusing on. Next, bring the zoomed-in image on the slide so the area of focus is now large enough to easily see. Finally, build your callout so the audience knows what you want them to understand about this portion of the screen capture.

For handouts, you can build all of this on one slide or you can have the full screen capture on one slide and then the builds on a new slide if a single slide would be too cluttered.

By zooming in on the area of focus, your point is more effective because the audience has context and can clearly see what you are pointing out.

Sample file available at samples.102PPtTips.com

Video available at www.PPtHowToVideos.com

Tip #50: What to ask for when having media clips created for you

When you hire a media company to produce media clips for use in your presentation, you will have to discuss certain parameters so that you get a file that is usable in your presentation. Most media clips are produced for broadcast usage and are too large to easily be used in your presentation. They can run slowly, or stop and start while playing. The result is a portion of your presentation being less effective than it could be. Here are some things to discuss with a media company when having clips created for you.

For audio clips, you want to receive the clips in the MP3 file format. This is a common compressed format and is easily played in PowerPoint while keeping the file size compact. There are two parameters that you need to discuss with your media contact. The first is the bit rate. It doesn't need to be as high as what broadcasters use. The sound system most presenters use is not nearly as good as what broadcasters require. If you have a bit rate of 128 you will usually be fine. The other parameter to discuss is the sample rate. A sample rate of 44,100 Hz is CD audio quality. If file size may be an issue, you can use a sample rate of 22,050 Hz and most people will not be able to tell the difference.

Video clips are usually more complex due to the addition of video parameters. The above audio parameters should also apply to the audio portion of video clips. The preferred file format for Windows PowerPoint is the WMV (Windows Media Video) format. This is something you need to insist on as most video editing is done on Macintosh computers that do not natively output to WMV files. If your media company gives you an

MOV file, the default from Macintosh computers, you will have to convert it (which usually results in a loss of picture quality), or play it outside PowerPoint because Windows PowerPoint does not support embedding this file type in a slide.

There are two important video parameters to discuss. The first is resolution. This refers to how big the video will be on the slide and is measured in pixels horizontally and vertically. A standard DVD is 720 x 480, and full HD video is usually 1920 x 1080. In most cases you can use DVD resolution on your slides. If you have a choice, see if 1024 x 768 resolution is available, as it will fill the slide (800 x 600 is a good second choice if computer screen resolutions are available). The second parameter that affects file size dramatically is the frame rate, measured in frames per second, or fps. The more frames per second, the smoother the video looks, but the larger the file size. Broadcast video is done at 30 fps. Most video clips will look just fine at rates as low as 10 fps. Ask to see samples of different frame rates to select the lowest rate that will look good.

When having media clips created for you, discuss these issues with your contact. Make sure they know you are using the clip in a presentation. Come armed with some knowledge of which parameters can affect file size and quality, and be open to discuss these items with them. Being better informed will result in a better experience for your audience as the media clip will run smoothly and illustrate the point you are making effectively.

Tip #51: Playing Flash or QuickTime videos in Windows PowerPoint

Windows PowerPoint allows you to insert many video file formats directly on the slide, but two popular formats are not on this list. The Flash format, usually an FLV file, and the QuickTime format, an MOV file, are not supported as video files that can be inserted on slides in Windows PowerPoint. There are add-ons that can convert the file format or there are programming techniques to play these files in a slide. Unfortunately, both options are usually far too complex for most presenters to deal with, especially if something needs to be fixed moments before a presentation begins. Here's an easier way to include these video files in a presentation.

Flash video is the most popular video format on the Web because virtually every browser has the Flash player installed and the video can play automatically on a web site. You may have a Flash video file that you'd like to use in your presentation. I think it is easiest to download a Flash video player program that plays Flash video files stored on your computer (one option I have used is the VLC media player at **www.videolan.org/vlc/** but others are available). Once you have installed the player application, you associate FLV files with that application in Windows Explorer. On your slide, create a hyperlink from a shape or text to the FLV file on your computer. When you activate the hyperlink in your presentation, the Flash video player will open and play the video. It is a good idea to expand the player to full screen mode by clicking on the button for full screen mode if it is available.

For QuickTime video files, you use a similar technique of linking to the MOV video file from a PowerPoint slide using the built-in ability of PowerPoint to link to outside content. Create a hyperlink from some text, shape, or picture to the MOV file on your computer. When you activate that link during the presentation, it automatically runs the movie in the Quicktime player (a free download from Apple that is probably already on your computer). When the movie is playing, you can expand it to full screen by pressing Ctrl+F. When it is done, exit the Quicktime player and you are back to your presentation.

For both file types, the appearance is not as clean as a video embedded on your slide because a separate player application opens up on top of your slides. But, in most cases, this is an easier technique than programming in PowerPoint.

Video available at www.PPtHowToVideos.com

Tip #52: Syncing audio with a set of slides is best done outside PowerPoint

PowerPoint allows you to add an audio clip to your presentation and it will allow the clip to play across multiple slides. This leads some people to try to coordinate a set of slides with a spoken audio track or a music track. It seems to work fine on your computer. But once you play it on a different computer, the synchronization is all off. What once promised to be an effective section of your presentation turns into a confusing mess.

The timing of slides changing or animation moving is dependent on many parameters of the computer, including the processor speed, memory size, and what other programs are running. All of this conspires to make properly syncing audio and slides in PowerPoint an almost impossible task. I suggest you don't rely on this technique and create a movie instead because it gives much more consistent results.

To start creating a movie with your slides, you need to first save each slide as a graphic file. PowerPoint makes this easy by providing a number of graphic file formats as options under the Save As file format list. I prefer the PNG or JPG file formats. When you select to save as one of these file formats, PowerPoint asks if you'd like to save the current slide only or all slides in your file. The easiest is to save all your slides since it eliminates having to save each one individually. Note that when saving as a graphic file, any animations will not work since it is like taking a photo of the slide when all animations have finished. So you may want to break some complex slides into multiple slides in order to show the builds one per slide.

Then, use a movie making program, like Windows Movie Maker, to import the images and the audio track. On the timeline in the program, add the audio track and do any editing to it so you know how long the entire presentation will be. Then, add each slide image in order in the video part of the timeline. You can adjust the starting time of the image and the length of time it is shown so that it lines up with the appropriate portion of the audio. You can also add transitions between the images, such as a fade between two images. Preview the movie to make sure it is what you want. Save the movie as a WMV file.

In PowerPoint, insert the WMV file you created as a movie on a slide. Set the parameters so that the movie plays automatically on the slide and it shows full screen. When you present the slides, the movie will play when you want it to and the synchronization will work every time, making your presentation more effective no matter what computer you are using.

Sample file available at samples.102PPtTips.com

Video available at www.PPtHowToVideos.com

Tip #53: Incorporate content from Word, Excel, PDF, or the Web

If you have information in documents or files from other programs that you would like to incorporate in your presentation, you can copy and paste the information or take a screen capture to show your audience. But you can also open that information right in the source program if it would be more effective to be able to scroll through it or interact with it during your presentation.

You have seen presenters do this awkwardly by exiting from Slide Show mode and manually opening another file. This disrupts the flow of your presentation, adds the potential for delays in finding the right file, and distracts the audience with all the other things they see on your computer. There is a much better way to open existing files on your computer.

The hyperlinking feature of PowerPoint takes advantage of Windows' ability to recognize a file format and open it in the correct program. In Windows, when you open a file, the system looks at the file type and automatically opens it in a program based on a list it uses for each file type.

To open a file from a different program, simply hyperlink to that file from text, a shape, or an image on your slide. When you activate the hyperlink during your slide show, the file will open in the correct program on top of your presentation (the file does not need to be opened and minimized before your presentation). You can use the program to demonstrate your point to the audience and, when you exit that program, you are returned to your presentation still in Slide Show mode as if you had never left it at all. It is seamless and not disruptive to the flow of your presentation.

This technique works for files in Word, Excel, PDF, or almost any recognizable format, as well as, web site URL's.

To make your movement to the hyperlinked file and back even more seamless, you can activate the hyperlink by using the Tab key during the slide show. When you press the Tab key, PowerPoint places a thin dashed line around the hyperlinked text or object. If you have more than one hyperlink on the slide, you can continue to press the Tab key to get to the desired hyperlink. Once the thin dashed line is around the correct hyperlink, press the Enter key to activate the hyperlink. Using the Tab and Enter sequence is equivalent to moving your mouse over the hyperlink and clicking on it, with the advantage that it is much less distracting for your audience. To exit most Windows programs and return to your slide show, you can use the Alt+F4 key combination. Test this before you present to make sure it works for the application you are using.

Sample file available at samples.102PPtTips.com

Video available at www.PPtHowToVideos.com

Tip #54: Inserting Excel data
that automatically updates

If you have to update slides with data from an Excel spreadsheet that changes regularly, you know how much time is spent re-keying the data and checking for transcription errors. There is an easier way. You can insert the Excel cells into your slide and have them update automatically when you open the slide show. Here's how.

First, format the cells in Excel exactly as you want them to look on your slide. Make sure you have set font size, borders, shading, and column or row labels in Excel.

Next, copy the cells in Excel and switch to your PowerPoint slide that has been created (usually a title only format works well for this type of slide)

Select to Paste Special in PowerPoint. In the resulting dialog box, select to paste this worksheet object as a link on the slide. Size the table if necessary on the slide.

Now, whenever the PowerPoint file is opened, it will ask you if you want to retrieve the latest data from the linked object. When you say, "Yes," it gets the latest data and updates the slide. This can save a lot of time if you have been manually updating data tables on slides from Excel worksheets.

One note of caution: If someone changes the name of the Excel file or moves the file, PowerPoint won't know and the updating will not happen because the source of the data can't be found.

Your presentation will be more effective when your slides always have the latest data for your audience.

Sample file available at samples.102PPtTips.com
Video available at www.PPtHowToVideos.com

Tip #55: Understand layering of elements on the slide

As you add elements (text, shapes, graphs, images, etc.) to your slide, each element is actually layered on the slide. This is not apparent until you try to move one element on top of another element. Then you realize that it is actually behind, instead of on top. The best practice is to think through the design of the slide before you start adding elements. Then add elements in the order that you want the layers to be in for the final look of the slide. If you need to, you can move elements forward or backward in the layers (towards the top or bottom of the layers).

To move an element within the layers, select the element first. Then, format the object and select to change the order or arrangement of the object (some versions of PowerPoint refer to this as the "order" and some use the term "arrange"). You have four choices:

- Move Forward which moves the object one layer forward. Use this once or multiple times to move an object in front of another object.
- Move to Front which moves this object in front of all objects. Use this when you want this object to be on the top layer.
- Move Backward which moves this object one layer backward. Use this once or multiple times to move an object behind another object.
- Move to Back which moves this object behind all other objects. Use this when you want this object to be on the bottom layer.

By understanding how layers work on a slide and how you can change what layer an object is on, it allows you to build slides that present your information in the way that will be most effective for your audience.

Video available at www.PPtHowToVideos.com

Tip #56: Don't forget the callout text when creating a callout

To focus the attention of the audience in any visual, you should add a callout that shows them where the most important part of the visual is and why this part is so important.

The first part of the callout is the graphic highlight. This is usually an arrow, circle, box, or some other graphic that is added to indicate where the audience should focus their attention. Most presenters use this well.

The second part of the callout is the callout text, and this is what too many presenters forget. The callout text explains to the audience why you added the graphic highlight. It explains why this part of the visual is so important that you highlighted it. Without the callout text, the audience won't know why they are supposed to look at the area being highlighted. And they may actually come to the wrong conclusion.

When you add the callout text, enclose it in a box or have the background of the text box shaded so that it stands out from the visual behind it. This gives it more prominence and makes it easier for the audience to see it.

> Click here to sign up

Graphic highlight (the arrow in this example) directs attention to the most important part of the visual

Callout text (enclosed in a box in this case) explains the importance of what the graphic highlight is pointing at

Tip #57: Use an emphasis animation effect to focus attention

Most presenters are familiar with animation effects that bring elements on to the slide. I suggest you build each slide item by item so you can explain each one individually and keep the attention of the audience. You can also focus attention with animation effects that emphasize certain elements of the slide.

Emphasis effects are used once the element has already been displayed on the slide. These effects serve to make the element more or less prominent. If you make it more prominent, the audience will place more focus on it. If you make the element less prominent, the audience places more focus on the other elements on the slide.

One of the best emphasis effects is the Grow/Shrink effect. It allows you to make an element either grow or shrink on the slide, depending on the percentage setting you set (greater than 100% is grow, less than 100% is shrink). I use a grow effect to make an image larger when I want it to be more visible, especially if the image contains text that I want the audience to be able to read, like in a screen capture. I use the shrink effect when I want to move an element to the background in order to emphasize another element while still having the first item on the slide for context. I might use it when I show a before and after sequence, and I will shrink the before item so that the after item is larger and we can spend time discussing it.

Other emphasis effects that may be useful are the ones that change the color of text (or lines), or change the size of the text. These can be used to emphasize certain parts of your slide after you have given context to all the parts together.

Sample file available at samples.102PPtTips.com

Video available at www.PPtHowToVideos.com

Tip #58: Use an exit animation effect to reveal underlying elements

If you need to build parts of a slide that the usual Appear animation effects won't work on, you may be able to achieve the same result using exit animation of overlying shapes. I have used this to reveal parts of a table of numbers, parts of a single graphic image, and parts of a graph.

The technique involves thinking in a different way. Instead of the normal approach of animating each element to come on to a slide, this approach reveals the elements that are already on the slide, but are covered up by other elements. It is like we used to do with overhead transparencies when we would cover part of the transparency up with a piece of paper and reveal each point by moving the paper.

There are two ways to implement this technique. The first is to begin by saving the background as an image. Then, add this image to the slide. Size it so that the image covers up the entire slide (it now looks like the slide has nothing on it). Use the cropping handles to crop the image to the desired size, covering up only the element you want to reveal later. In the animation task pane, apply an exit animation to this image so that when you advance, the image is removed from the slide, revealing what is underneath.

The other way to implement this technique is to use the transparent background method I first saw demonstrated by PowerPoint MVP Glen Millar. I find this usually easier to use than the first method. This method uses the ability to fill a shape with the background of the slide. First, draw a shape, for example a rectangle, on the slide, covering up the element or portion of the element you want to reveal. Format the shape so that it has no outline and the fill effect is set to Background. If you are covering up a graph or other element that has a background different from the slide (like a white background on a graph or imported image), set the shape color to the background of the underlying element. Again, animate this shape so that it exits when you advance on this slide. Using either approach, you can achieve the building of the elements on the slide in the order that you want to discuss them in.

The only downside to this second method is that when you print the slide, the shape or image covers up the other element and it appears that there is nothing there on the slide. To get around this, create a duplicate hidden slide that does not use this technique and print this hidden slide instead of the slide you use for presenting.

This exit animation technique will allow you to build your slide element by element even if the regular Appear animation technique won't work exactly the way you want it to.

Sample file available at samples.102PPtTips.com

Video available at www.PPtHowToVideos.com

Tip #59: Use a motion path animation to illustrate an idea

Sometimes making something move on the slide explains your point better than you could with words. Motion paths allow you to move an object from one specific spot to another on the slide. How can this help? Let me give you two examples that illustrate how I have used this technique to improve the effectiveness of a slide.

When I was speaking to accounting professors at a conference, a motion path allowed me to show a number moving from one spot in the general ledger to the appropriate spot in the T-account. It doesn't matter if you don't understand the accounting terms. Showing the number move on the slide instead of just having the number appear in a new spot was exactly what their students needed to see in order to be able to use the knowledge later on. Using a laser pointer or pointing with my hand would have been even more confusing. If you need to show how an item gets from one spot to the next, motion paths can do a better job than any other method.

In showing a manufacturing process, you could show a product moving from one stage in the process to another. This can be far more effective than just showing the steps or trying to describe them. If the process involves transportation of the product to a different facility, you can also have a train or truck moving between facilities. In this way, you almost create a movie, but without the expense and hassle usually associated with video production.

The next time you want to show movement of items on a slide, use motion paths to make the point more effectively.

Sample file available at samples.102PPtTips.com

Video available at www.PPtHowToVideos.com

Tip #60: Overview of using copyrighted material on your slides

Many presenters use copyrighted material in their presentations, but not everyone understands how to use it properly. This overview is intended to help you identify when you may want to seek more advice on using a copyrighted piece of work. This is not intended to be a legal opinion and you are advised to seek your own legal opinion before you proceed in these areas. Having said that (for legal disclaimer purposes), here are some areas to keep in mind.

Copyright generally covers any original expression of ideas. This expression can be in many different formats, including cartoons, books, music, videos, photographs, movies, audiotapes, written works, drawings, artwork, speeches, and slides. Regardless of how the format is represented, whether in a physical form such as a printed book or CD, or in electronic format such as a graphic file or MP3, the copyright still applies. Regardless of where the item is stored, whether in a home, office, or on the Web, the copyright still applies. And even if the copyright symbol (©) is present or not, the copyright still applies.

Any time you use a copyrighted work, you must have permission from the owner of the work. The author or creator of the work may not be the owner of the work, so you must be careful in determining the true owner of the work. To use their work, you must have written permission to do so. The owner may ask how you want to use their work and how many times you will use it before they decide on how much they will charge you in order to use the work. In some cases, certain uses will be allowed and others not permitted for the same copyrighted work.

Consider all possible uses you may have for the work before you approach the copyright owner so that you can negotiate an agreement that is fair for both parties.

Depending on the type of copyrighted work, the process for getting permission to use the work is different. With some items, such as written works, drawings or photographs, you will usually have to negotiate directly with the copyright owner. For many media works, such as recorded music or videos, there are licensing organizations that may be able to grant you usage rights for the work you are seeking or a blanket license for all works that they license. You will have to do some investigation to see which applies to the work you want to use.

Arranging use of a copyrighted work will involve some time and effort on your part. One alternative is to create your own copyrighted work that you can use as many times and in any way you want. There are now many freelance cartoonists, poets, and musicians who will create a work according to your specific needs and assign you all rights after you pay them a reasonable fee. Check the Web for these sources of material.

Using copyrighted material can be effective in your presentation, as long as you obtain the appropriate permission in advance and respect the rights of the owner of the work.

Tip #61: How to use the non-visible area of a slide

When you read the topic of this tip, you may be wondering what the "non-visible" portion of a slide refers to. Don't worry, most presenters aren't aware of it or how you can use it to make your slides more effective.

The non-visible portion of a slide refers to the area around the slide that is not actually seen when the presentation is displayed. You can still use it, and the advantage is that the audience will not see what you put there. Why would you want the audience not to see something? Let me give you two examples.

First, if you are adding an audio clip to your slide, by default, PowerPoint will place an audio icon on your slide, sometimes right in the middle of the slide. While you can move the icon to a corner of the slide, the audience can still see it and it can be distracting. Instead, move the icon to the non-visible portion of the slide by moving it off of the slide area. It will still play like it always has, but the audience won't be distracted by the icon on the slide.

Another use is to create effects where an object comes on to the slide from one of the sides of the slide. Let's say you want a truck image to move on to the slide as if it is coming into view when you are looking out the window. By placing the truck image in the non-visible area of the slide, you can then make it appear to be moving onto the slide with an animation effect.

In general, the non-visible area of the slide is useful any time you want to hide something from the audience's view, whether you end up bringing it onto the slide or not.

Sample file available at samples.102PPtTips.com

Tip #62: How to create a scrolling list of credits effect on a slide

To recognize a group of people for their accomplishments in a presentation, scroll their names and what they are being recognized for across the screen. This will look like a scrolling list of credits similar to what you see at the end of a movie. You won't need to use the built-in animation effect that comes in PowerPoint because there is a more effective technique.

Start by creating a list that contains the names and accomplishments in a text box. Make sure that the font size is large enough, perhaps 32 point or larger. Position this text box below the visible portion of the slide.

Next, apply a motion path animation to this text box to bring it vertically from below the visible portion of the slide to above the visible portion of the slide. This will move the text box vertically through the visible portion of the slide, making it look like it is scrolling the text box.

You will need to adjust the timing of the motion path animation because the default will be much too fast. You can set the speed parameter of the animation to a fixed number of seconds instead of one of the preset values. You may need 30, 60, or even more seconds depending on how fast you want the names to appear and the length of the list.

You can have other graphics on the slide during the credits to make it look even better, or you can use the traditional basic black background. This technique will be effective for recognizing individuals during your presentation.

Sample file available at samples.102PPtTips.com

Tip #63: Create a menu to run a day of presentations without ever dropping out of Slide Show mode

If you are organizing a day of presentations, keep in mind that it is awkward for the audience to see one presenter exit their presentation and then have to watch the next presenter find their file and start it up. This "exit and start" method is distracting and disrupts the flow of the presentations. Instead, set up a menu for the day that allows sessions to flow smoothly from presenter to presenter.

You can create a menu slide using PowerPoint's ability to hyperlink to another PowerPoint file. First, create a new file and design a slide that has a list of the presentations for the day. You may even design it like an agenda for the day listing times, titles, and presenters' names.

Copy each presenter's presentation file to the same folder that you have stored the menu slide in. If the presenter sends you an updated version of their file, simply copy it over the old version of the file.

Beside each item in the list on the menu slide, draw a small rectangle and set the color and outline of the rectangle to No Color and No Line (this creates a transparent shape that can't be seen but is still an element on the slide). Create a hyperlink from that rectangle to the appropriate presentation file that you have saved on your computer.

During the day, all you have to do to start a new presentation is activate the hyperlink beside each presentation name on the menu slide. The appropriate presentation opens up and the presenter is ready to go. They can use PowerPoint as if their presentation was the only one running.

When they are done, press the Escape key to end their presentation and you return to the menu slide, ready to select the next presentation. What if the presenter arrives at the start of the day with a new version of their file? No problem. Just copy the new file over the existing file before you start the day and the hyperlink still works.

This technique will make the day more effective for the audience because the flow of information from one presenter to the next is maintained without distracting interruptions. This makes it look more professional and polished.

Video available at www.PPtHowToVideos.com

Tip #64: Protect slide content
so it can't be changed

Sometimes you need to create a PowerPoint presentation in such a way that others cannot change the slide content. This may be for legal reasons where you don't want a disclaimer or other text removed from the presentation. Or it may be that you don't want a graph or other visual altered that could misrepresent the information. This may be particularly important when the presentation is distributed and viewed or delivered by others.

Some versions of PowerPoint have ways to restrict file access using somewhat complicated methods that often require additional software to be installed. In many cases this is a burden and there is an easier way to get almost all of the same benefits. It uses the ability of PowerPoint to save a slide as a graphic. Here are the steps to use this technique.

Step 1 – Create your slides in PowerPoint as you normally would, with all the graphics and text you need. Proofread and review your slides to make sure they are finalized.

Step 2 – Save the slides as graphic files. To do so in PowerPoint, use the Save As function to save all or just one of the slides as a PNG graphic file (one of the formats listed in the dialog box).

Step 3 – Create a new presentation that consists of the images, each sized to fill the slide. The slides will look exactly as before, but since the entire slide is an image, no elements can be changed on the slide.

You can use this process to make all of the slides unchangeable or you can use it just for selected slides. You may leave some of the text slides as regular slides and only protect the graphs or tables of data that should not be changed. If you use builds on your slides, where text or graphics are displayed as you advance through the slide, making the slide an image removes those builds, so think about what portions of the slide you need to protect. You can protect an underlying graph, then add text boxes on top of the image to retain the ability to build ideas on a slide.

Using this technique will allow you to give other presenters the flexibility they need to customize each presentation, while protecting important data that needs to be left unchanged. They can add to the images, but the important sections that need to remain will still be there.

A slightly different type of protection may be required when using photos that you have cropped in PowerPoint. Even though the cropped areas of a photo are not displayed on a slide, those areas of the photos are still stored in PowerPoint. Someone can uncrop the photo to see what you have cropped out, which may be a problem in some cases.

To protect cropped photos, you can use an option in the compress picture function. Instead of compressing the picture, only select the option that allows you to delete the cropped areas for this picture. The resulting photo looks the same but has the cropped areas deleted, and someone won't be able to see what was cropped out.

When protecting your slides will assure that the correct message is delivered, use these techniques to protect the content of your slides.

Sample file available at samples.102PPtTips.com

Tip #65: Web based presentations need to be designed differently than in-person presentations

If you haven't delivered a presentation using a web conferencing service, you will soon. Travel budgets are being cut and you will be holding more meetings virtually instead of in person. A presentation you would give in person won't always work well when delivered over the web. Here are some changes you should consider when designing presentations that will be delivered over the web.

Eliminate movement effects: While web conferencing has come a long way technically, one of the functions it doesn't handle well is movement of objects on the screen. Those moving arrows or fancy transitions between slides will look jerky and the whole point of the movement will be lost when delivered over a web conferencing service. The hesitation in the movement is created by the delay in transmitting what is happening on your screen to all the participants. Cut out the movement and use simple animations, such as items simply appearing on the slide, or the next slide appearing in place without movement to get there.

Don't show video clips: One of the hottest trends in presentations is to use videos. Unfortunately, when presenting over the web, video streaming doesn't work well. Most videos shown on the Internet are not streamed in real time like a presentation is. They are downloaded to your computer and played locally. Instead of having your video show poorly, convert that slide to a picture of the person speaking and the most important quote they make in the video. If you want the audience to view the video after the presentation, post it on your web site and direct them to it with an e-mail link after you are done.

Use callouts to direct attention on visuals: If you would normally point to a spot on the slide in a live presentation, your audience on the web won't be able to see where you are pointing. Use a callout instead that consists of two parts. The first is a graphic highlight (like an arrow or circle) that directs the prospect's attention to a certain spot in the visual. The second is the callout text to explain why that spot is so important. Adding callouts is also essential if you send a copy of your presentation to those who could not attend the presentation.

Design interactivity to keep their attention: In a live presentation, you can get feedback by looking at the audience's faces and body language. You lose that opportunity for feedback and interaction with a web presentation. So you must design interaction for your web based presentation. Keep the audio line open so you can hear them and include open ended questions that probe their thoughts on a topic, their experiences with an issue, or how they would answer a particular question. This interaction keeps them paying attention and not surfing the web or checking e-mails.

Web-based presentations can be effective if you keep in mind some of the differences with live presentations. Design slides that will look good when transmitted through a web conferencing service.

Tip #66: Clean out old or ineffective slides on a regular basis

Like most professionals, you are an expert in your field and you are asked to speak on the same or similar topics frequently. To save the time of recreating all your slides from scratch, you have a file that you usually use and it works pretty well. Let me encourage you to throw some of those slides out. Why? Because I know (and you do, too) that you have improved your presentation since those slides were originally created and you know there are more effective ways of presenting certain points. Throw out the slides that don't work and create new slides. Your whole presentation will be more effective as a result. Here are some reasons to eliminate and change slides in your presentation.

As you have been presenting, you may get the sense that you are going into too much detail. Most audiences want the conclusion, not all the data behind it. Watch your audience when you cover really detailed parts of your presentation. Are their eyes glazing over? If so, adjust the detail level to match your audience. Cut out detail for most situations and add it only when speaking to certain audiences.

Are there areas where you are presenting similar information about two topics? It might be similar policies for two situations or similar features for two products. If so, cut one set of slides and consolidate the information, saving you time in your presentation and saving your audience from hearing similar information twice.

Where should new or updated information be added in your presentation? Always be looking for opportunities to update existing slides with the latest results, or add new slides based on new research or new information. If the data on a slide is outdated, stop using it. The audience places no weight on information that is not current, so don't diminish your effectiveness by using outdated information.

Lastly, make sure you are finishing your presentation on time without rushing through the last part of the presentation. Going over time or rushing through is a sign that you have too much in your presentation. Pare it down to just the essential information your audience needs to know. Make sure you have built in time for interaction and questions, whether during or after the presentation. A comfortable pace is more effective than rushing through too much information.

Sometimes the best way to increase the effectiveness of your presentation is to cut some of it out.

Tip #67: Incorporating other slides
Step 1: Fix the layout

I have seen so many presenters struggle with incorporating slides from other presentations, their own or from colleagues, that I've decided to give you three tips on how to make this process easier. By cutting the time spent incorporating other slides, you have more time to work on making the overall message more effective.

The first step is to check the Slide Layout of the existing slides. This is the one area that causes more problems than almost any other area. Unfortunately, most presenters don't know that they should select the appropriate layout when they create a slide. They just use the default bullet point layout and delete or move items until they get the slide they want (see Tip #27 for suggestions on selecting slide layouts).

The problem is that once you incorporate that slide into your presentation, PowerPoint applies your design to the inserted slide and uses the underlying layout to move the slide elements back to where they are supposed to be, according to your design. This causes you to have to manually move the elements on the slide to where you want them to be.

So, before you reformat or insert any slides, review the layouts and apply or reapply the correct layout to each slide. You may also need to move text from randomly placed textboxes into the correct placeholders so it will format properly when inserted into your presentation.

Video available at www.PPtHowToVideos.com

Tip #68: Incorporating other slides
Step 2: Fix the Slide Master

The second area you need to check before merging slides into your presentation is the Slide Master. The Slide Master controls the colors, fonts, and placement of title and body text, as well as, any branding such as logos or graphics. PowerPoint uses the information on the Slide Master to reformat any inserted slides, so getting it set up properly will save you a lot of time later on (see Tip #26 for more on the Slide Master).

Too often Slide Masters are poorly constructed simply because designers or presenters aren't aware of the benefit of using a Slide Master or the best practices for creating a Slide Master. Look for and fix the following:

- Background colors should be set on the Slide Master and not set by using a colored rectangle on each slide
- Background graphics should be on the Slide Master and not on each individual slide
- Title and body text placeholders should have the correct font, size, alignment, and color set on the Slide Master and not individually on each slide
- Footers and slide number placeholders should be properly formatted and set to display if desired
- Animation effects should not be set on the Slide Master or else they will apply to every slide.

By checking and fixing the Slide Master before inserting any slides, you eliminate a lot of the reformatting that usually needs to be done.

Video available at www.PPtHowToVideos.com

Tip #69: Incorporating other slides
Step 3: Copy and Paste then Fix

You are now ready to incorporate other slides into your presentation. If you need to, open a new presentation and apply the design from the Slide Master you fixed in the previous step. Next, open the existing presentation and copy the slides into the newly formatted presentation, allowing the new design to be applied automatically (don't select the option to keep the formatting from the original slides). This will correct most problems, but some will still exist (it seems to be inconsistent sometimes).

Since not everything will be corrected automatically, check each slide and reapply the layout if needed. You may also need to make some final fixes to the position of elements due to background graphics that may be in a different position in the new design.

Initially, it sounds like the pre-work will take some time, and indeed it will. But it is my experience that the time to complete the pre-work is much less than the time to correct all the problems manually. Be efficient incorporating slides so you can spend more time making the content and delivery as effective as you can.

Video available at www.PPtHowToVideos.com

Delivery

You can have the greatest slides ever created, but poor delivery will undermine all the work you've done so far. Deliver confidently with these tips on equipment setup, fixing problems that occur, stage techniques of the pros, and how web presentations differ from having the audience in front of you in the room.

Tip #70: Practicing and Rehearsing are not the same thing

If there is one thing presenters could do in the area of delivery that would help them improve, it is to prepare more effectively. I know it has made a big difference in my own presentations. To prepare effectively, you should budget the time to both practice and rehearse. Yes, they are two different things.

Practicing is what most presenters consider as adequate preparation. They sit in front of their computer and run through their slides. They look at the slides and think of what they are going to say. This is good and necessary to make sure the sequence and content is correct. But it is not adequate to prepare you for a live presentation.

You must also rehearse. Rehearsing is actually standing and delivering your presentation as if it was in front of the audience. It is the only way to make sure that what you are planning to say on a certain slide flows smoothly and fits the slide as designed. If you can use the room and equipment that you will be using for your presentation, you can become comfortable with the setting and the equipment. If you are using a different room, try to picture the actual meeting room when rehearsing. Pretend that an audience is in the room and practice making eye contact with different audience members. Time yourself so you know if your presentation is too long or too short.

By practicing and rehearsing, you give your presentation the best chance to be effective. Why don't more presenters do both? I think it is because they don't set aside the time for rehearsals. Rehearsing requires you to plan and set aside more time, but is well worth it to make your future presentations more effective.

Tip #71: Test these things at the office and on site before you present

What do you think when you see a presenter with spelling errors on their slides, linked files that don't work, or images that appear blurry? Like me, you probably start to lose interest, or think less highly of the presenter and their message. You can reduce the probability of these types of problems happening in your presentation by checking the following at the office and in the meeting room thirty to sixty minutes before you begin to speak:

- Check the spelling on each slide by reading the words in reverse order and getting someone else to read the slides for you
- Run through the animation sequence to make sure everything appears when it is supposed to
- Activate every hyperlink and make sure that it works properly
- Play every audio and video clip to make sure it plays and the volume is audible
- Check all projected images to make sure they look crisp and clear when shown on a large screen
- Check all special symbols that you have used to make sure that the operating system and PowerPoint version are still displaying the correct symbol.

By checking these items before you present, you are more assured that the presentation will run smoothly.

Tip #72: Equipment to carry when presenting

When I travel to deliver customized workshops or speak at conferences, I carry the normal equipment for a presenter: my laptop, presentation remote, and projector if required. In this tip, I want to share with you a few of the other pieces of equipment I carry that come in handy when travelling.

The first item I carry is a VGA extension cord. Mine is 15 feet long. It allows me to move my laptop away from a lecturn or projector. Too often, A/V people position the cord to connect the laptop to the projector in places that cause a problem as a presenter. One common setup is the cord taped to a lecturn. I never use this setup because it creates a barrier between the audience and myself. The other common situation is a short cord right beside the projector. The problem with putting your laptop beside the projector is that the laptop can overheat from the hot air blowing out of the projector. A VGA extension cord allows the laptop to be in a more convenient position and makes the session more comfortable for the speaker and the audience.

The second item I carry is my wireless mouse. One reason I carry it is because when I am working in a hotel room, I find it much more comfortable to use a mouse than to use the touchpad on my laptop. I use a wireless mouse instead of a retractable wired mouse because it can then also serve as a backup for my presentation remote. If my remote fails, I can use my wireless mouse as a substitute until I can replace the remote.

The final item I carry is a small travel alarm clock. It is easy to set and use. I use it in two ways. First, when I am in my hotel room, I always use it to wake up in the morning. If you stay in as many hotels as I do, you don't have time to figure out all the alarm clocks and you learn not to trust them. So I know I'll always wake up on time if I use my own. Second, when I am presenting, I set it to the local time and sit it beside my laptop. This way, I always know what time it is, even if there is no clock in the room or the time on the clock in the room is wrong (happens often around the change to/from daylight savings time). It makes sure that I can manage my time during the presentation, questions, or exercises, and we finish on time.

None of these items are high-end technically, but they are three of the most useful items I carry with me when I present.

Tip #73: Arrive early to make sure the setup works and to get to know your audience

If you have tested your presentation before you arrive, why do I still suggest you arrive at least thirty to sixty minutes before your presentation? Because it allows you to address two areas that can't be dealt with until you are present in the room that you are presenting in.

First, you can look at the room arrangement and see if there are any changes that need to be made in order to make your presentation more effective. Are there lights right above the screen that are washing out the image? Ask the facility staff to turn them off or remove the light bulbs. Does everyone have a clear view of the screen? Walk to the sides or corners of the room to see if part of the screen is blocked. Sit in the chairs and see how much of the bottom of the screen will be blocked if there are people sitting in front of the person sitting in this seat. See if there are changes that can be made or certain sections that should be taped off. Is the screen a great distance from the last row of the audience? If so, you may need to increase the font size of any text so that it can be easily read by the people at the back of the room.

Once you are set up, you want to have time to meet the audience members as they arrive. Start to build a relationship with them by asking them what their interest is in your topic, what they are hoping to get from the session, or what their biggest challenge is in your topic area. Visiting with the audience before you start improves your effectiveness two ways. First, they are already warmed up to you, so they are more inclined to trust what you are saying. Second, you get a pulse of the room and can anticipate any issues that may get raised.

Tip #74: Know how to set up
your computer with a projector

It used to be that setting up a laptop with a projector was easier because the resolution of both machines was the same. But with laptop resolution now much higher than the resolution of most projectors, this connection has started to cause problems. Many projectors can't handle the high resolution, or try to display it and it ends up distorted or looking strange. Here are my suggestions for reducing the issues when connecting a laptop to a projector.

First, toggle your laptop so that the display is on both the laptop screen and the projector. This is usually accomplished by a function key combination. The display on the projector may not look good at this point, but that's OK.

Second, use Windows to change the resolution of your laptop to match the native resolution of the projector. The resolution setting is usually found in the Control Panel. You should set it to 1024 x 768 unless you are certain that the projector can handle a higher resolution. This usually corrects a number of projector display issues because the aspect ratio now matches, and the projector isn't trying to compress a high resolution image.

Finally, set the Slide Show display resolution in PowerPoint to the same 1024 x 768 resolution. This ensures that when you switch to Slide Show mode, the resolution stays the same and the image is still good.

These steps won't solve every problem that may happen, but they will go a long way to solving the most common issues.

Tip #75: Know how to fix
media clips that won't work

When you are testing your presentation on site, what do you do if one of your media clips doesn't work? There are a number of potential problems, so let's work through them step by step.

First, check if the video file exists. Too often, people think that PowerPoint embeds the video file into the presentation, but it does not. PowerPoint only links to the video file, so the video file must exist on the computer in order for it to run. If the video file does not exist on this computer, you will have to get it or decide to present without the video.

If the video file does exist, or you were able to get a copy of it, see if it will play in a media player, such as Windows Media Player. If the video has an error playing in the media player, the file is likely corrupt, and you will need to get a new copy of it or decide to present without the video. If the video file does play correctly in a media player, then you can re-insert the video file on the slide in your presentation. On the slide, delete the old video link and re-insert the video file. Set the options and re-test to see if it works.

In rare situations, an inserted video file does not play. One option is to create a hyperlink to the video file on your slide. Activate the hyperlink when you are presenting and your default media player will play the video. It won't look as nice, but at least you can use the video.

If none of these solutions work, hide the slide with the video on it and present without the video. Going without the video isn't ideal, but at least you discovered the issue before you started, instead of during the presentation.

Tip #76: Set up before you display your screen on the projector

Too often, the first thing presenters do when setting up is connect their laptop to the projector. Unfortunately everyone can see what they are working on before the presentation starts, since the image is now also being projected on the big screen in the room. This is distracting for the audience members who have arrived early, and the presenter risks the embarrassment of having something private displayed for all to see.

Instead, do all the setup you need before displaying your laptop screen through the projector. The safest approach is to not connect the display cable to your computer until you are ready to show the audience what is on your screen. Some laptops automatically detect the cable being connected and immediately display the screen whether you want it to or not.

The other option is to use the display toggle function of your computer and set it so that only your laptop screen is displayed. This way, you are the only one who can see what is displayed even though the computer is connected to the projector.

When you have closed the other work and started your presentation, you are now ready to show the audience your screen. Plug in the display cable and use the toggle function to display the image on both your laptop screen and the large screen in the room. You may have some final resolution adjustments to make, but that can't be avoided as most times the available resolutions are not known until the computer and projector are connected (see Tip #74).

Make sure you avoid embarrassment and audience distraction by displaying your screen only when you are ready to begin your presentation.

Tip #77: Set up a pre-presentation loop as a hyperlink

Some presenters like to have a loop of slides running before their presentation starts. These might be housekeeping or other announcements, humorous images, calming photos, interesting facts, or trivia that keep the audience interested and anticipating the presentation. The challenge comes when it is time to switch from the pre-presentation slides to the presentation slides.

Since the pre-presentation slides are in one file and the presentation slides are in a different file, many presenters exit the first file and start up the second file. But this is seen by the audience and it breaks the atmosphere that has been created by the pre-presentation slides. There is a better way to switch between slide files that is smooth and seamless.

You can hyperlink from a shape to start a new PowerPoint file from within a slide show that is already running. Let's walk through how this would work to run a loop of slides before your presentation.

First, add a blank slide at the start of your presentation. Draw a rectangle on that blank first slide and set the line and fill colors to No Color so the shape can't be seen by the audience. Next, add a hyperlink to the shape that opens the PowerPoint file containing the loop of slides.

When you start your presentation file, the first slide will look blank to the audience, but it contains the hyperlink that opens the slide loop file. Activate the hyperlink and the looping slides will appear and start playing. When it is time to return to your presentation slides, simply press the Escape key to end the looping presentation and you are back at the blank first slide, ready to move to the second slide to start your presentation.

Video available at www.PPtHowToVideos.com

Tip #78: Don't complain about the room, setup, or A/V in front of the audience

It is rare that everything is set up perfectly for your presentation. The room may not be configured properly, the temperature may be too warm or cold, the projector may be a little old, or any number of other things may be less than ideal. Knowing that many things could be an issue, it is always a good idea to arrive early to deal with it (see Tip #73).

The one thing you should never do is complain about the situation in front of the audience. As a presenter, your job is to do the best with what you have to work with. If you complain about the situation, the audience may not sympathize with you. It is possible that they will think poorly of you for complaining and be less receptive to your message even though someone else may be the one responsible for the room and setup.

If there is a situation that is an obvious problem, like the temperature in the room being at one extreme or the other, you need to acknowledge the situation and let the audience know what you and the facility staff are doing about it. Have backup strategies that can help alleviate the impact of some of the potential issues, like the suggestions in Tips #81 and #82.

There will be many issues you face as a presenter that you have no control over. Just try to remedy the situation and be honest with the audience about those issues that impact them. They will be understanding and open to what you have to say.

Tip #79: Use a presentation remote

I recommend that you build your slides point by point and build the visuals piece by piece so you can focus the audience on each part of your message. When you do this, you will quickly find that you are tied to your computer to advance each build unless you use a presentation remote.

A presentation remote allows you to advance your builds and slides without having to be physically close to your laptop. There are many models of remotes available, ranging from simple ones that just provide movement of slides up to ones that allow full mouse control and even have timers to track how long you have left in the time allotted for your presentation. They work by having a receiver attached to a USB port on your computer and the remote in your hand communicating with the receiver to transfer your commands to the program.

I suggest that unless you really need full mouse control or the other features, you stick with a simple version of a remote. The Interlink Remote Point Navigator that I use only has four buttons: forward, backward, blank the screen, and a laser pointer. I don't need more than those functions.

When I started bringing my remote with me, one helpful tip I learned from professional speaker Ed Rigsbee was to remove one or both batteries from the remote before you pack it in your computer case. This way, a button won't get accidentally pushed when in the case and drain your batteries (yes, this has happened to me).

Once you use a presentation remote and see how much more effective you are as a presenter by using it, you'll wonder why you went so long without one.

Tip #80: Stop using a laser pointer

Why are laser pointers a problem for many audience members? Here are five reasons:

1. Many people can't see the small dot of a laser pointer on the screen due to its size and the lighting in the room.
2. It is virtually impossible to hold a laser pointer exactly still, and the movement on the screen naturally distracts people to look at the movement instead of listening to you.
3. The only way to hold the laser dot in the correct place is to face the screen, but then you end up speaking to the screen instead of the audience.
4. People who get the presentation by e-mail later don't know what you were pointing at and don't even know when you were using a laser pointer.
5. People viewing the presentation over the web/video link can't see what you are pointing at since they aren't in the room to see the laser dot.

Instead of using a laser pointer, design your slides with callouts that you build one by one. Callouts allow you to face the audience the entire time, don't distract with movement, are big enough to see, and are part of the slide so anyone viewing the slide over the web or later will know what your callout was pointing to.

As I suggested in Tip #56, make sure your callouts have a graphical highlight that points out the important part of the visual and callout text that explains why that part is so important. Callouts add to the effectiveness of your slides in the presentation when presented live and when viewed later.

Tip #81: Know how to respond when equipment stops working

I have said many times in the past that it is only a matter of "when" you run into equipment problems during a presentation, not a matter of "if" you will run into problems. If you haven't had equipment fail on you just before or during a presentation, just wait, it will happen one day. The effectiveness of your presentation depends on how you handle any of these problems that arise. Here are my suggestions.

Most importantly, you must commit to still delivering your message. The audience came to hear your message and you have a responsibility to deliver it. This mindset is key in whatever you end up doing to resolve the problem or if you resort to a Plan B.

When equipment fails, look for obvious causes, such as someone tripping on a cord and pulling it out, or batteries dying in a remote. Address the obvious causes and see if that solves the problem. If there are no obvious causes or if those solutions don't work, call a five minute break to see if the next approach will work. Shut down and restart the equipment (computer, projector, etc.) and see if it works now. You have only about five minutes to do this before you move on to Plan B.

Plan B is how you finish the presentation without your slides. Give this some thought before you present because it may happen to you. Some strategies that I've used: use any other visual mediums available to create visuals, such as flipcharts, blackboards, or whiteboards; use the handout that you have given the audience as a guideline and reference tool; and, use your arms to draw the key visuals in the air (remember that you have to draw it from the audience's perspective, which takes some practice to do properly).

By preparing for possible equipment failure, you can prepare contingency plans that you can use before moving to a Plan B. Some presenters carry a second laptop or copy their file to a USB stick as a backup that can be run in another laptop. Some presenters carry a backup projector to use if the primary one fails. And some presenters carry a wireless mouse as a backup if their presentation remote stops working (as discussed in Tip #72). Contingency plans can cost money as you invest in backup equipment, and some of the backup plans may force you to bring extra luggage if you are travelling. Consider the risk/reward tradeoffs before investing in backup equipment.

If you handle equipment failures with grace and calmly move on to finishing your presentation, the audience will hardly remember any problems because they will focus on the great content you presented.

Tip #82: Know what to do when you have less time to present than you thought you did

The organizer tells you at the last moment that you have less time to present than you thought you did. How do you handle this? The most common approach from presenters is to speed up the pace of speaking and rush through all the slides anyways. This is not effective because the audience feels like they are only able to grasp a few of the many ideas rushing past them and they miss most of the information.

Instead of trying to cram everything in, take a step back and decide what the most important ideas are that you should share. Go to your slides and hide those slides that don't relate to those most important ideas. Don't delete the slides, because you want to be able to go to one of the slides if the audience asks for more information on that topic. Present this abbreviated set of slides so that your presentation fits in the time you now have. If the audience has a handout of all your slides, just let them know when you start that you have included more slides for their further review after the presentation, but you will only be highlighting the most important slides during your time with them. You can indicate where the current slide is in their handout if you feel that is necessary.

Another approach is to let the audience decide what the most important areas are in your presentation. Make a quick note of the slide number for your agenda slide and the first slide of each key section of your presentation (this is why having a presentation map as explained in Tip #7 is so important). When you present your agenda slide, tell the audience that you have prepared a number of topics to discuss and because of the limited time you would like them to determine which topics you will present. Let them select the most important topic. To jump to the start of that topic in your presentation file, simply key in the starting slide number on your keyboard and press the Enter key. When you are done that topic, return to the agenda slide by typing in the slide number for the agenda slide and pressing the Enter key. Move through the topics in the priority that the audience tells you and finish whenever your time is up. Again, you can direct the audience members to the appropriate page in the handout as you move to different topic areas.

You are more effective when you keep a reasonable pace and cover only the topics that are of greatest importance to the audience. The audience and the organizer of the presentation will be thankful that they can keep on schedule when you finish on time.

Tip #83: How to handle mistakes on your slides

Sometimes as presenters we make a mistake on a slide and someone notices during the session. Often the mistake gets discovered because the explanatory text on the slide and what the presenter said were not consistent with what the visual showed. This happens to all presenters, no matter how careful we are. The key is how you respond when someone points out the mistake.

Unfortunately, this seems to rattle some presenters. If you are a little nervous, this could throw a big wrench in your wheels. But don't worry. It is actually a good sign when people are asking questions like this because it shows they are interested and have a desire to better understand your point.

So what should you do? First, pause a moment to determine whether what they are saying is correct. You may even want to ask them to explain what they see as incorrect because you may not be able to see the error. This can get other audience members involved and it can provide additional insight that everyone can benefit from.

If indeed your slide is incorrect, admit the mistake, using humour if possible. In a recent presentation, I immediately recognized that I had indeed made a mistake and handled it by saying: "I did that just to see if you were paying attention!" People laughed and I apologized for the mistake. If you are not sure whether the information is a mistake, be honest and say that you are not sure about it; let them know you will investigate more and get back to them. If you did make a mistake, ensure the audience knows the correct information, and move on to your next point.

Don't dwell on the mistake and don't beat yourself up over it. We all make mistakes from time to time, and your audience understands that. They are just glad it didn't happen to them that day.

Tip #84: What you should do instead of looking at the screen when you are presenting

What is more important when you are presenting, looking at the screen or looking at the audience? Obviously looking at the audience. So why do so many presenters look at the screen when they present? Whether it is nerves or habit, it doesn't make for an effective presentation. What should you do instead? Here are some suggestions.

First, position the laptop so you can see the laptop screen from where you will be standing when you present. If you need to glance at the screen to see what the next point is, glance at the laptop screen instead of turning around to the screen on the wall. If you can't position the laptop so you can see it from where you are standing, turn your head briefly so you can see the screen, turn back so you face the audience, then begin speaking. Don't speak while you are facing the screen.

Second, if you are relying on the slides as speaking notes, you need to rehearse more and you should start using visuals. By rehearsing more, you will be more comfortable with the material and you will not need to constantly be looking at the screen to know what to say. By using visuals, it forces you to stop relying on text notes and start telling the story that explains the graph or visual, which is more effective anyway.

Third, if you are facing the screen because you are nervous about facing the audience, you need to become more comfortable with speaking and presenting. Join a local Toastmasters group or attend a public speaking course that can help you become comfortable speaking in front of an audience.

Videotape yourself presenting or have a trusted colleague watch to see if you are facing the screen when speaking.

Tip #85: Properly introduce a photo or video before showing it

Often a presenter will show a photo or video and then explain what the audience was supposed to get from it. Wrong order. Without context, the audience creates their own conclusion and your explanation is lost. It may even result in someone raising their hand and asking you to replay the video or show the photo again because they don't understand your point.

To be more effective, properly introduce a photo or video before you show it on the screen. You must give context to the photo or video before displaying it. Otherwise, the audience does not know what point is being made and may be lost, or even worse, come to a different conclusion.

In your introduction to the visual, explain what the audience will see and what they should be looking for that illustrates your point. With a photo, give the context such as location, time, or situation and tell the audience what they should look for in the photo. For a video clip, explain why you are showing the clip, what it will be showing, and when during the clip they should pay the most attention to catch the important point.

For example, if I am introducing a video testimonial, I might say, "I'd like you to hear from Denise Stewart, the plant manager of the Main Street factory. Listen about 15 seconds in as she describes the reduction in employee turnover they have experienced because of this training program. Let's watch this clip." Now your audience knows why they are watching the clip and how it illustrates a key point you made.

Tip #86: To highlight a spot on the slide, draw on the slide

Before PowerPoint was projected, a common visual aid was the overhead transparency. You could display a pre-printed transparency, and you could also write on it, or even use a blank sheet and create your own visual by drawing on it. Many presenters would like to be able to write on their slides sometimes to illustrate a point. You can do this in PowerPoint. Here's how to draw on your slide in Slide Show mode.

1. Press Ctrl+P (hold the Control key and press the P key) to turn the cursor into a pen cursor. You can right-click and select pen options such as type of pen, color of ink, and thickness of line.

2. Use your left mouse button to draw on the slide as you would in a drawing program. This is usually easier to do with a mouse than with the trackpad on a laptop. It also takes practice to make the drawing look smooth. Some presenters prefer a drawing tablet or a touchscreen laptop to give better control.

3. If you want to erase a portion of the drawing, press Ctrl+E to change the cursor to an eraser cursor. This eraser removes entire lines, not portions of lines, so be careful using it and practice before you present. Press Ctrl+P to change back to the pen cursor. If you want to erase everything you have drawn, press the E key.

4. When you are done drawing, press Ctrl+A to return to the regular cursor, and press A to hide the cursor. When you exit Slide Show mode, the program will ask if you would like to save what you have drawn on the slides. This can be helpful if you are capturing input or discussions with

the audience and want to have the drawings for distributing to others after the presentation is over. The drawings get saved as simple line objects on your slides and can be edited later.

Drawing on your slides is not something that you will do in every presentation, but it is good to know that you can if you need to. It increases the effectiveness of your message when you can customize a slide or capture ideas without disrupting the flow of your presentation (see Tips #9 and #53 for other ways to capture ideas in Word or Excel).

Video available at www.PPtHowToVideos.com

Tip #87: To jump to any slide, use one of two methods

Most PowerPoint presentations will be delivered in a linear manner, starting at slide 1 and proceeding to the last slide. In Tip #9, I talked about designing non-linear presentations that improve the engagement of the audience. Even if you haven't designed your presentation to be a non-linear one, you can still jump to any slide in your file using one of two techniques.

First, if you know the slide number you want to jump to, simply enter that number using the numeric keys on your keyboard and press the Enter key. This jumps to that slide without the audience seeing the slides that were skipped over. This is useful if you know the slide number of your conclusion slide and need to jump straight to it because of time constraints. It is also useful when you want to display a prepared slide that you have saved in case a certain question gets asked. Jump to the prepared slide to answer the question, then jump back to the slide you were on.

The second method is not as seamless as the first. In Slide Show mode, press Ctrl+S to bring up a list of all the slides in the file. It lists the slide number and the title of the slide if there is one. You can select any slide in the list and click the Go To button to jump to that slide. The audience will see you do this, but it may be acceptable if you have good rapport with them and they appreciate your flexibility in presenting what they want to see at that moment.

By being willing to jump around in your presentation, you demonstrate that you are flexible to the audience's needs and you increase the effectiveness of your message.

Video available at www.PPtHowToVideos.com

Tip #88: How delivering web based presentations differs from in-person presentations

If you haven't been involved in designing and delivering presentations over the web yet, it is an important skill to learn. With businesses having a global scope and travel budgets being reduced, more meetings will be virtual instead of in-person. Here are some best practices when delivering web-based presentations.

Use a second PC as a participant: No matter how fast your web connection is, or how fast the connection of each participant is, there will always be a slight delay between when you show the next slide and when they see the slide on their screen. By the time the service takes your new slide, transmits it to the system's server, and then sends it out to each participant, anywhere from one to several seconds will elapse. The challenge is that you will not know when the participants are seeing the new slide unless you set up a second PC on your desk and connect that PC as a participant. Then you can advance to the next slide and keep transitioning with what you are saying until you see the new slide on the "participant PC." This way, your speaking can always match the visuals that your participants are seeing.

Use a standard screen resolution: Many computers today come with high resolution monitors that can be quite large. Even laptops have wide screens that can show full HD resolution videos. But in almost all cases, the higher resolution will hurt instead of help your presentation. A 1680 by 1050 widescreen monitor has almost 2.25 times as many pixels as a normal XGA resolution of 1024 by 768 (which is the resolution of most projectors). That means that the web conferencing service will have to send 4.5 times as much data each time (2.25 times from your computer to the server and 2.25 times from the server to the participant). This means much slower load times for each slide and longer waits for the participants to see the next slide. And what if the participant doesn't have a high enough resolution on their screen? Your well-designed visual may appear distorted or even not appear at all. It is best to reduce the resolution of your screen to 1024 by 768 (or something close), so that the slides appear quicker and look crisp on each participant's screen. You can always change the resolution back after the web meeting is done.

Use callouts instead of drawing tools: One feature that the web meeting services offer is the ability to use drawing tools during your presentation. Most of the services allow the presenter to grab a virtual pen or highlighter and draw on the screen. While this sounds like it would be a great idea, be careful. Movement is very hard to show smoothly during web meetings. Too often your drawing of a circle around an important concept or highlighting a key phrase will look jerky to the participants. This jerkiness makes the participants think that something isn't working properly or they missed something – both distract the participant from your message. Instead of using the drawing tools, create proper callouts that direct the attention to the important spot on the slide (see Tip #56 for more on callouts).

As you start to replace in-person presentations with web presentations, keep these best practices in mind. You will find the presentations more effective and you will reach your objectives faster.

Video available at www.PPtHowToVideos.com

Tip #89: What to look for in a web presentation service

What should you look for in a web presentation service in order to improve the effectiveness of your presentations that are delivered through this method? I've done web presentations for years and here are some of the factors I suggest you consider when selecting a provider of web presentation services.

1. Select a service that supports both Windows and Mac computers. Some of your audience members may be accessing the service from home and they won't be using the corporate standard hardware you are used to.

2. Select a service that allows you to share your desktop instead of restricting you to content that you upload in advance. This increases your flexibility and makes your presentation more effective.

3. If possible, use a service that provides audio connections via either telephone line, or through the microphone and speakers on the computer. Give your audience members flexibility in the way they access the audio portion of the presentation.

4. Make sure that audio mute is available on both your end and the participant end. In noisy locations such as a factory, airport, or busy home, being able to mute an audio line makes the presentation better for everyone.

5. Use a service that allows you to switch presenters during the presentation. It allows you to include others in delivering the information. It even allows you to pass control to a participant who wants to show a particular issue or situation on their own PC, so that everyone can discuss it and help.

6. Match your intended usage to the pricing structure of the service. Some services are free, but offer limited features. Some services charge per participant per minute that they are connected. And some services charge a flat monthly fee. Find a service that will match your intended usage pattern the best.

There are many services available. This list of criteria will allow you to narrow down your choices to the one or two services that best meet your needs. Selecting the right service will help you make your web-based presentations more effective.

Video available at www.PPtHowToVideos.com

Tip #90: Creating a presentation that runs automatically when opened from an e-mail

When you send a presentation to someone by e-mail, the default method is to open the presentation in the basic PowerPoint editing mode. The disadvantage is that the person may never view it in Slide Show mode, so all builds or movement animations are lost when they view it. There is a more effective way to distribute presentations that gives the recipient a better experience when they open the presentation.

The method relies on saving your presentation in a slightly different file format than usual. The default PowerPoint file format is PPT or PPTX (for version 2007 and above). This opens in editing mode by default. If you choose to save your presentations in the PPS or PPSX PowerPoint Show file format, it will open in Slide Show mode by default. Then the recipient of the file can walk through your presentation seeing all the builds in order and any other animations that help explain your points.

You can take it the next step by utilizing some of the features available in Slide Show mode to create a unique experience for the viewer. You can set up the show to automatically advance through some introductory slides as soon as the file is open. It can then display a menu of options that the viewer can select with their mouse and customize the presentation to what they want to see. This is a non-linear presentation that is created using hyperlinks on the menu slide. Now you have an interactive presentation that is delivered uniquely to each person viewing it.

Utilizing the PowerPoint Show file format increases the effectiveness of presentations you distribute by e-mail.

Video available at www.PPtHowToVideos.com

Tip #91: Keep track of what works

At a professional speakers convention, one of the keynote speakers, Darci Lang, shared an idea that has helped her improve her presentations. She said that one of the things she does after every presentation is to take a few minutes to note down in a journal what went well during that presentation and what didn't work so well. This is an important practice for presenters to follow. Here's how I would adapt it when applying this technique to your slides.

When using PowerPoint slides, take note of the expression you see on people's faces when they see the slide. If they are confused, it may be a signal that the slide is not designed as clearly as you thought it was. This doesn't mean that you should necessarily go and change the slide for your next presentation. The benefit of noting it in a journal is that you can see patterns emerge.

If you note that a slide didn't work well and see in your journal that this is the third note about that slide, it is a trend suggesting that the issue is with the slide, not the audience. After you make a change to a slide, track whether the new slide is working or whether further changes are necessary. Use the trends that appear as a more reliable indicator than the reactions of a single audience. You will end up with a better reading that way.

As presenters, we need to use the feedback from our audiences to help us improve. Then we can be more effective communicators when using visuals.

Handouts

If you want your audience to remember what you said and apply it, you will want to leave behind documentation that helps them recall your key points. These tips will show how you make handouts effective tools in your presentation, and even how to deal with the situation when you are not allowed to use a printed handout.

Tip #92: Design handouts so the audience pays attention to you

I am a strong advocate that presenters use handouts when they are presenting. There are many ways to design a handout though. One common question is, "Should your handout be a copy of your slides, or not?"

It depends on what you want the audience to do with the handout. In most presentations that I see, the handout is there as a reference for the audience during the presentation and a reminder after the presentation. If this is the case for you, I suggest using a copy of the slides as a handout.

By having a printout of your slides in front of them, the audience is reassured that they already have your key points. This allows them to focus on listening to you and understanding what your message means to them.

I also suggest having space around the slides in your handout so that the audience can take notes. Why would they need to take notes? Because you want them jotting down how they are going to use your ideas in their own situation. If they have no room to take notes, they won't be able to capture their thoughts on how they want to apply the ideas.

I usually use the four slides per page handout layout in PowerPoint. It gives space around the slides that the six slides per page format does not give. And it allows people to take notes around the slides instead of restricting them to lines beside the slide, as the three slides per page format does.

By designing your handout so that it benefits your audience, your presentation will be more effective.

Video available at www.PPtHowToVideos.com

Tip #93: Format your handout to add consistency and aid recall

PowerPoint allows you to set up a consistent look for all handout pages in the Handout Master similar to the consistent look you create for slides through the Slide Master. I suggest you add three pieces of information to the Handout Master.

In the top left corner, add the name of your presentation. Why should you add the name on every page if the first slide probably has the name on it already? Because if the pages get separated, and they will, the name is always there. Your audience members will pull the handout apart to give certain pages to others for follow-up, file each section with related information, or share the information with those who did not attend. This way, everyone who receives a page will know or recall what the topic of the presentation was.

In the lower left corner, I suggest you include a copyright notice, if appropriate, and your contact information. Your contact information can be a web site address, e-mail address, or phone number. Again, you want everyone who sees any page of the handout in the future to know how to get in touch with you.

Finally, in the lower right corner, add the page number with text in front of the number such as "Page". You can be more descriptive such as "Slide Handout Page" if you have multiple handouts and want to easily distinguish them. The text and page number make it clear what the number refers to.

Now every page of your handout will have consistent branding and, even if they get separated, each page has information that will allow someone to recall the topic and get in contact with you if they have a question.

Video available at www.PPtHowToVideos.com

Tip #94: Why you may not want to include every slide in your handout

While I suggested that you use slide printouts as a handout, you will want to consider whether the audience needs every slide in your file. You can easily select which slides are included in the handout and the order they are printed, by specifying those parameters when you print the handout.

One reason you may want to exclude a slide is that there are times where you duplicate a slide when you are building a visual or idea. Perhaps only the last slide in a series of two or three is all that the audience needs. In this case, exclude any of the slides that contain the partially built visual so that the audience is not confused.

Another reason to exclude a slide from the handout is that by including it, you would give away a surprise you have planned during your presentation. For example, you may have a humorous visual that adds a laugh in the presentation and, by including it in the handout, it would give away the punch line. Just leave that slide out of the handout.

Choose to leave certain slides out of your handout. You will still have a useful handout and an even more effective presentation.

Video available at www.PPtHowToVideos.com

Tip #95: Make black and white printouts look good

Color printing is more expensive than black and white printing, so most handouts are printed in black and white. If your slide has a coloured background, the default settings will cause the printout to use a lot of ink or toner. The default setting, which is called Grayscale, attempts to convert every color to a shade of grey. This results in the slide background being a shade of grey which uses excessive ink or toner.

The common solution used by many organizations is to make the slide background white, so that it does not get converted to a shade of grey. This is not necessary and it may reduce the effectiveness of your presentation, as it may cause you to change other colors, and lose the organizational branding on your slides.

Instead, set the Color/grayscale setting in the Print dialog box to "Pure Black and White". This option converts the background to white, all text to black, and any images to grayscale. Even if you have a dark slide background, your printout will have a white background, and look clean and easy to read. It also saves a lot of ink or toner when printing.

Video available at www.PPtHowToVideos.com

Tip #96: If you need to have a detailed handout, use hidden slides

Too often, presenters pack slides with too much text and information. They justify these crowded slides by claiming that the audience needs to have the detail in the slide handout for future reference. But what happens is that the barrage of information on the slide overwhelms the audience and the presentation is not effective.

One possible solution many presenters suggest is to put the reference information in the Slide Notes section, and provide the PowerPoint file so the audience can read the Slide Notes later. Unfortunately, most people don't know this section exists since it is so small on the screen. So using the Slide Notes isn't a good solution.

There is a better way. Instead of overloading information on your slides, design a slide file with both detailed slides and properly designed visuals. This file can serve both show and print purposes. Here's how you can do it.

For each topic, create two slides. The first one you will display during the presentation. This should be a visual slide, not packed with text. The next slide should contain any detailed information you want the audience to refer to after the presentation. This second slide will never be shown during the presentation. It is there for printing purposes only.

Hide each of the detailed slides. This stops the detailed slide from being seen during the slide show. When you are running your slide show during practice sessions, make sure that the detailed slides are not shown.

To print a handout of slides that includes both the display slides and the hidden detail slides, check the Print hidden slides checkbox on the print dialog box. You will then get a printout with each of the detailed slides beside or below the display slide. Your audience can quickly see that they have more detailed information and can take notes that are appropriate to their own situation.

When you are presenting using this type of handout, it is a good idea to mention how the handout is structured at the start of your presentation. This lets the audience know that they do not need to take copious notes and can be more engaged in what you are saying. It also frees you from feeling that you have to plow through a lot of detailed slides in order to finish on time.

If you do want to display one of those detailed slides during the presentation, you can access it using the two methods described earlier in Tip #87 for jumping to any slide. Even though they won't display during the normal running of the slide show, the hidden slides are still in the file and can be displayed if you need to.

The hidden slides are also a good reference for anyone who did not attend and receives the slides via e-mail after the presentation. The detailed slides allow them to have all the information they need to understand your message.

When you want your audience to have detailed information, keep it off the slides you show, and use the hidden slides approach to make your presentation more effective.

Video available at www.PPtHowToVideos.com

Tip #97: Use Word to create speaker notes or a detailed take-away

If you need to create a handout that is more than the slides and may include speaker notes or other information, consider using Word to design and format the handout. PowerPoint makes it easy to get images of the slides into Word so you can combine the slides with other content.

There is a built-in function in PowerPoint that will allow you to export all the slides into Word. You select the format to use. You can select whether the slides are each on their own page or grouped, and whether lines or blank areas are under each slide. The advantage to this method is that it is automatic and creates a document that you are ready to edit.

You can also use the Save As function of PowerPoint to save each slide as an image file (the PNG file format works well). In Word, you can import any of the slide images, and position or size them as needed. While this gives you more flexibility in creating the handout document, it is a little more work to actually get the slide images into the Word document.

With a handout created in Word, you can format it and add other content that is not on the slides. You can use Word to format the pages with borders, headers, and footers that are more flexible than the options found in PowerPoint. You could add content such as a list of references for additional information, notes for presenters who are delivering the presentation or any other content that will make the handout a better presentation reference for your audience. Make sure that the handout sequence still fits with the presentation sequence so the audience can easily follow along when you are presenting.

Video available at www.PPtHowToVideos.com

Tip #98: Use a PDF file to make your handout more robust

More and more presentations or handouts are being distributed in PDF format so that they can be viewed on any system and look the same. I always provide my clients with a PDF handout so that when they print it, I know it will look the same as when I created it. Those who receive the PDF file can then easily e-mail it to others who did not attend the presentation.

This tip gives you four ideas on how you can make a PDF copy of your presentation be more than a simple printout of your slides. Note that these ideas require you to have a full copy of Adobe Acrobat (not just the free Reader application), or the ability to create and edit PDF files in another application.

If you want to have your audience (and I use the term audience to mean anyone who is opening the PDF file to review it) look at more information on a web site, add a hyperlink to a slide. There are two steps to this. First, on your slide, incorporate a hyperlink to a shape or text and add text that gives an indication that a hyperlink is there. Second, in Acrobat, use the Link tool to add a rectangular hyperlink area to the shape or text on that slide. Now, when the audience wants to use the hyperlink, they can see the hyperlink and click on it in Acrobat. This will take them to the web page with more information.

One great advantage to creating a distributable version of your presentation in PDF format is that you can combine a printout of your slides with other documents that are in PDF format. These documents could be detailed spec sheets, performance data or financial information. Multiple PDF documents can be combined using the Insert Pages feature to create a single presentation package that you can e-mail out.

If you do decide to create a combined document PDF file, one concern is that the page numbering won't be consistent, since each printout will number its own pages starting at page 1. You can solve this problem by not adding page numbers in each source document. Then, in Acrobat, use the Add Headers and Footers feature to add page numbers, copyright information and any other text you want to each and every page. The page numbers start at 1 and flow throughout the combined PDF document regardless of the source document.

The final idea is to attach reference files to the PDF document that you think people might want to use or refer to. You can use the Attach a File feature in Acrobat to attach pretty much any type of file as part of the PDF file. If you have a spreadsheet that you want them to fill out in order to see the magnitude of an issue, attach it and create an instructions page so they know how to find the attachment and use it. This increases the usefulness of the presentation for each person who opens the PDF file.

When you have to distribute your presentation, use these ideas to create a PDF version of your presentation that is much more than just a slide printout. It can be a consistently branded document that links to relevant information on the web, and contains interactive components that make it more valuable and effective.

Tip #99: Why you should give handouts to the audience before you start

One of the most contentious questions I get when it comes to the topic of handouts is: "When do you give out the handout - before or after you speak?"

Some will argue that you always give it out after you speak. They say that if you give it out before, people can read ahead and know what you are going to say. If everything you are going to say is on your slides, this is true. But my philosophy is that your slides should be visuals that guide a conversation with the audience, not a transcript of everything you are going to say.

So my suggestion is to give a handout before you speak. I have three reasons for suggesting this. First, it gives your audience somewhere to take notes that are relevant to them. Every audience member will take something slightly different from your presentation. They need somewhere to jot down those ideas while you are speaking or they will forget by the time you are done.

Second, if they know they have a copy of your slides and other relevant material, they can pay more attention to what you are saying. They don't need to be concerned with trying to madly write down what is on your slides. Too often people get very frustrated at the end of a presentation where they have spent considerable energy writing down key points from the slides only to be told that they can pick up a handout on the way out.

The third reason I suggest you give a handout before you speak is that it serves as your backup in case your technology fails. As I explained in Tip #81, your handout is one of the components of your Plan B for dealing with equipment failure. If the audience doesn't have the handout, you won't be able to use this key instrument in recovering from a problem with your presentation equipment.

You should not be concerned about people looking through your handout before you speak. As long as the handout is well designed, the audience will appreciate having it up front because it helps them better understand and apply your message.

Tip #100: Creating a handout for hearing or sight impaired audience members

There is no reason that an audience member who is vision or hearing impaired cannot understand your message. The key is to create a handout that is useable by the technology that is available to assist them. Hearing impaired audience members will need to be able to read additional detail that closely follows what you are saying. Sight impaired individuals will need a document that their computer can translate into speech that they can listen to. You can create a single Word document that serves both purposes.

For most slides, simply adding notes in the Slide Notes section of the slide as explanatory text to what is on the slide is the biggest step that needs to be taken. After these explanatory notes have been added, the slide is output to Word in a format that each slide is a page in the Word document. Each page has the slide number at the top, an image of the slide (similar to a screen shot), and the explanatory text below the slide. This is one of the default export formats from PowerPoint. This Word file is saved and is provided as the handout.

The Word file satisfies the requirements because it provides an image and text that can be resized for visually impaired people, it provides a text description that deaf people can read, and the text can be read by a screen reader program which is support for the assistive technology used by blind or visually impaired people. This method is easy to produce and easy for the end-user to use.

By converting your handout to this format, it is useable and effective for audience members with vision or hearing impairments.

Tip #101: What to do if you are not allowed to use a handout

A recent trend as part of the environmental efforts of organizations is to ban handouts for presentations. The challenge is how to deal with the potential downside of this policy – decisions being made on poorly recalled ideas and facts because the audience is splitting their concentration between what you are saying and writing notes.

Let me suggest an approach to designing and delivering your presentation that has a high potential to get the key messages remembered and acted upon in this no-handout scenario. It involves planning in a slightly different way and delivering your presentation in a somewhat more direct manner.

Step 1: Plan your key messages even more carefully

I have always advocated a strong and clear structure as the foundation of any presentation. Without a handout to guide the audience, you need to place an even greater emphasis on the clarity of the structure and defining each key point that you will make. This is important because you will be directing the audience to make note of these key messages as you deliver your presentation. A good way to test your structure is to write out what you want the audience to have in their handwritten notes at the end of your presentation. Then you need to design your presentation to ensure that they find each of those points so compelling that they write them down.

Step 2: Design slides with a headline and visuals

The more text the audience sees on the slide, the less they are inclined to write it down because they can't figure out what the important point is. Instead, design each slide with a headline that summarizes the key message and a visual that engages the audience in a conversation with you. If there is an easy sentence or point for them to jot down and they are engaged in understanding the importance of that point, they are more likely to write it down and remember it.

Step 3: Manage their expectations

Your audience may not know what to expect in terms of how much they need to write down and whether they will be able to catch everything you say. This can cause extra tension on their part. You want to ease that tension so they can hear and understand your message. To do so, let them know at the start of the presentation how things will run. Let them know that you'll be indicating the key points to remember, that they can take any notes they want that are relevant to them using the information you will be sharing, and that you'll make your slides or a sheet of notes available via e-mail after your presentation. This way, they are relaxed and ready to listen to what you have to say.

Step 4: Tell them what to write down

As harsh as this sounds, if you don't give them direction to write certain points down, they likely won't write down what you want them to. Here are some examples of phrases you can use at different points in your presentation:

"I think you will want to write this down/note this/jot this down"

"Make a note of this"

"Jot down this point"

"This is a keeper"

"You will want to share this with others/refer to this later"

Use variations on the above phrases to direct the audience to write down what you want them to remember from your presentation. If you have prepared them in advance as stated in the previous point, no one will take offense to these reminders.

Step 5: Reinforce at the end and after the presentation

At the end of your presentation, make sure you have a slide that summarizes the key points you want to make sure they have noted. You can again use a reminder to prompt those who may have missed a point to make note of it. You could say, "On this slide, I've summarized the key ideas we have discussed today. You may want to take a moment to make sure you haven't missed any of these in your notes so that when making your decision, everyone has the same set of facts." Base this slide on the ideal set of notes you started with in the design phase. If you have the e-mail address of everyone in the audience or the contact information of the organizer who knows everyone who attended, you can distribute your slides or a key points summary document by e-mail later that day or first thing the next day. You want to get this reminder of the key points in their hands within 24 hours, if possible, so that it locks your messages into their memory.

With more organizations looking to be environmentally friendly, you will more frequently run into the restriction of not being allowed to use handouts in your presentation. When faced with this potential obstacle, use the ideas above to design and deliver an effective presentation that will still get remembered and acted upon.

The Last Tip

The best way to end this book is to give you direction on where you can go if you have more technical questions. The resources in this tip will steer you in the right direction to find the answer to almost any PowerPoint question you may have.

Tip #102: Where to get PowerPoint help

As you gain more experience with PowerPoint, you will increase your knowledge of how to accomplish most tasks. But where do you go to figure out a question that you don't know the answer to? Here are the sources I use for technical help.

First stop is the PowerPoint FAQ list at **www.pptfaq.com**. It is created and maintained by Steve Rindsberg, one of the Microsoft PowerPoint MVPs. If you are having a problem with PowerPoint or are wondering how to do something specific, chances are Steve or one of the other MVPs who contribute have already written an article on it.

If it has to do with an error message or a technical issue, I head over to the Microsoft support site at **support.microsoft.com**. This allows you to narrow your search to the version of PowerPoint you have and search for any articles on the problem or issue. It also links to downloads of service packs and other updates that can help solve problems.

Many of the PowerPoint MVPs (experts recognized for their contributions to increasing the knowledge of the user community) have web sites with helpful tips. One of the most extensive is **www.indezine.com**, run by Geetesh Bajaj. For a list of all of the MVPs and their sites, go to **www.mvps.org/links.html#PowerPoint**.

You can always search Google or your favourite search engine for information on the issue you are having. I have found I get better answers when I include the version of PowerPoint as a search term and make the search as specific as possible. When you get a whole list of possible pages to look at, which ones should you give preference to? I usually look for pages from the site of an MVP (see link to list above) and those at educational institutions, since they tend to have good online help pages for their staff and students.

The final destination I want to share is the PowerPoint newsgroup. When you need to ask a question and want it answered by an expert, head over to the PowerPoint newsgroup (**microsoft.public.powerpoint** in a newsgroup reader or through Google groups). Here you can post a question or search for previous answers that may have covered your question. It is best practice to search for previous answers first as there tend to be common questions that come up on a regular basis.

I wouldn't expect that any one individual will know all the answers to every PowerPoint question (although some of the MVPs come pretty darn close). By using the resources above, you can find the answer to a question you have and increase your knowledge of PowerPoint.

Conclusion

You will probably see the best results if you start by using the two or three tips that you think will make the biggest difference in your next presentation. Then, as you become comfortable with using those ideas, start to use a few more in future presentations. And, as you use more and more of the tips, you'll see your presentations be even more effective.

Not every tip will apply to the presentations you do today, but the world of presenting is changing, and you will likely be able to use many of these tips in the future.

As colleagues notice the improvement in your presentations, encourage them to get their own copy of this book so they can experience the same success you have in your presentations. One by one, we can help improve PowerPoint presentations for audiences everywhere.

Index

6 x 6 guideline, 60
Adobe Acrobat, 154, 155
Agenda, 19, 105, 131
Align, 71, 72
Alt+F4, 92
Animation, 8, 37, 54, 60, 61,
    62, 70, 79, 84, 89, 97, 98,
    99, 100, 103, 104, 118
Annoying PowerPoint Survey,
    8, 9
Audio, 56, 85, 89, 90, 103,
    110, 118, 142
Bajaj, Geetesh, 163
Billiondollargraphics.com, 67
Bit rate, 85
Black slide, 33
Brain Rules, 26, 27
Branding, 47, 48, 49, 50, 51,
    114, 148, 150
Bullet points, 25, 46, 51, 60,
    61, 113
Callout, 43, 68, 83, 84, 96,
    110, 128
Cialdini, Robert, 55
Color contrast, 40
Compress photographs, 75,
    108, 122
Context, 17, 31, 61, 68, 69, 81,
    84, 97, 136
Copyright, 101, 102, 148, 155
Credit list slide, 104
Crop, 70, 83, 84, 98
Ctrl+A, 137
Ctrl+E, 137
Ctrl+P, 137
Ctrl+S, 139
Display toggle, 122, 124
Distribute, 71, 72, 144, 155,
    161
Draw on the slide, 137

Dual-Coding Theory of
    Cognition, 64
E-mail, 23, 25, 26, 68, 73, 75,
    110, 128, 144, 148, 154,
    155, 160, 161
Emotion, 56
Emphasis animation, 97
Ending a presentation, 35
Engage the audience, 22, 23
Equipment problems, 129,
    130, 156
Escape key, 105, 125
Excel, 91, 92, 93, 138
Exit animation, 98, 99
File type
    FLV, 87
    JPG, 47, 78, 89
    MOV, 86, 87
    MP3, 85, 101
    PNG, 47, 89, 107, 153
    PPS, 144
    PPSX, 144
    PPT, 144
    PPTX, 144
    WMV, 85, 90
Fill effect, 99
Flash, 87
Follow-up, 26, 148
Font, 42, 43, 44, 45, 49, 61, 93,
    104, 114, 121
    Arial, 43, 44
    bold, 61
    Calibri, 44
    italic, 61
    Times Roman, 44
    underline, 61
Font size, 42, 43, 93, 104, 121
Frame rate, 86
Freehand drawing tool, 78
Gantt chart, 72

Training, Consulting & Resources

If you want your sales presentations to get better results, your project proposals to get acted upon, and your training workshops to make changes in behaviour, contact me about a workshop that is customized to your team. We work on customizing the content for your specific needs, and I use your slides as makeover examples so you see the ideas applied to the slides you actually use. We can cover structure, sequence, slide design, slide content, and delivery. Just call me and we'll discuss how to set up a workshop that helps your entire team.

When you need help with a specific high-stakes presentation, I can help you from deciding on the strategy for the message through creation of the visuals to preparing for delivery. Contact me and we'll discuss how to start the process.

I offer many resources on my web site, including my book, *The Visual Slide Revolution*, videos, articles, the newsletter, and more. You can also follow me on Twitter (@daveparadi) or connect with me on LinkedIn to keep updated with my latest writing and events.

Phone: (905) 510-4911
E-mail: Dave@ThinkOutsideTheSlide.com
Web: www.ThinkOutsideTheSlide.com

Book Recommendations

Made to Stick by Chip Heath & Dan Heath
ISBN 978-1-4000-6428-1 – available at all bookstores
(published by Random House)

Influence by Robert B. Cialdini
ISBN 978-0-06-124189-5 – available in bookstores (published
by Harper Collins)

Multimedia Learning by Richard E. Mayer
ISBN 978-0521735353 – can be ordered through a bookstore or
online book seller (published by Cambridge University Press)

Brain Rules by John Medina
ISBN 978-0979777745 – can be ordered through a bookstore or
online book seller (published by Pear Press)

Bulk Book Orders

When you see the difference these tips make in the success of your presentations, you will want a copy for every member of your team. Discounts are offered when you order ten or more copies. Here is the discount schedule:

1-9 copies $29.95
10-25 copies $24.95
26 or more copies $19.95
(actual shipping cost will be added to your order total)

To place your bulk order, fill out the form below and fax it to (905) 826-2410, or call (905) 510-4911 to place your order by phone. Payment options include credit card, corporate or government purchase order, or check. We will call to confirm payment method.

Name: _____

Company: _____

Address: _____

City: _____ State/Province: _____

Zip/Postal Code: _____

Telephone #: _____

Number of books to order: _____

Individual Book Order

You know how much the tips have helped your presentations, why not order a copy as a gift for a colleague or friend. Fill out the form below and fax to (905) 826-2410 to order a copy today.

Name: _____

Address: _____

City: _____ State/Province: _____

Zip/Postal Code: _____

Telephone #: _____

Credit Card information (VISA or MasterCard only)

Card #: _____

Expiry Date: _____ / _____

Cost of each book is $29.95 plus $3.50 for shipping and handling.

You can also order online at www.102PPtTips.com.